AIDS

TO THE STUDY OF

GERMAN THEOLOGY

BY THE

REV. GEORGE MATHESON, M.A. B.D.

AUTHOR OF
'GROWTH OF THE SPIRIT OF CHRISTIANITY'

THIRD EDITION

WIPF & STOCK · Eugene, Oregon

Wipf and Stock Publishers
199 W 8th Ave, Suite 3
Eugene, OR 97401

Aids to the Study of German Theology, 3rd Edition
By Matheson, George
ISBN 13: 978-1-60899-951-4
Publication date 9/21/2010
Previously published by T & T Clark, 1877

TABLE OF CONTENTS.

INTRODUCTION.

Aim of the Treatise—Comparative untroddenness of the field—Inadequacy of verbal translation to meet the difficulties of the student—Proposed remedy for this inadequacy—Pre-Kantian Theology—Relation of the German mind to Rationalism and Romanism—Brief sketch of the downward progress of Rationalism from Leibnitz to Semler—Relation of Kant to the systems of Rationalism, ... 1

CHAPTER I.

THE NATURAL THEOLOGY OF KANT.

Ontological argument stated—Kant's criticism of it—Examination of that criticism—Relation on this point between Kant and Hegel—Wherein consists the value of Kant's criticism—Cosmological argument stated—Kant's criticism of it, and examination of that criticism—Statement of Teleological argument—Kant's criticism of it examined—Relation here existing between Kant and Hegel—Kant's attempt to reconstruct by means of a moral argument—Examination of that attempt, and of the cause of its failure—Kant's theological position, ... 12

CHAPTER II.

KANT'S INTERPRETATION OF THE FACTS OF SCRIPTURE.

Kant's interpretation of the Fall—of the possibility of redemption—of the conditions necessary to redemption—of the nature of God—of the Trinity—of revelation—of the Person of Christ—General summary of his theological merits and defects, ... 23

CHAPTER III.

TRANSITION TO SCHLEIERMACHER.

Immediate effect of the Kantian scepticism—Consideration of the two opposing tendencies to which it gave birth—Two forms of the tendency to rest on faith apart from reason—Frederick Schlegel—Jacobi—De Wette—Schleiermacher—His intellectual characteristics and theological position—Inquiry into the cause of his influence—Distinction between Schleiermacher as a religious thinker and as a scientific theologian, 33

CHAPTER IV.

THOUGHT-TRANSLATION OF THE SYSTEM OF SCHLEIERMACHER.

Schleiermacher's view of the nature of God—of the attributes of God—of the creation of Man—of the Fall—of the Person of Christ—of redemption—of the completed Trinity in the Church—General summary of his theological merits and defects, ... 41

CHAPTER V.

DIVERSITIES IN THE SCHOOL OF SCHLEIERMACHER.

Consideration of the points of difference between Schleiermacher and his disciples as exhibited under the following heads:—
1. Nature of God; 2. The Trinity; 3. Attributes of God; 4. Immortality; 5. Origin of Evil; 6. Person of Christ; 7. Redemption, ... 58

CHAPTER VI.

FICHTE.

Tendency to anarchy—Relation of Fichte to the philosophy of Kant—Legitimacy of his deduction—Leading idea of his system expounded and defined—His five stages—Examination of these stages—Later modification of his view—Inconsistency between his creed and his character, . . . 72

CHAPTER VII.

INTRODUCTION TO THE THEOLOGY OF HEGEL AND SCHELLING.

Relation of this theology to the Kantian contradictions—Its relation to the philosophy of Fichte—Unity of the theology of

Schelling and Hegel—Prevalence of their idea in previous systems—Diverse views as to the interpretation of their theory—Necessity of divesting the mind of prejudice in considering this subject—Adjustment of the comparative merits of Schelling and Hegel in the construction of their system, 82

CHAPTER VIII.

TRINITY OF SCHELLING AND HEGEL.

Difficulty of the subject—Fundamental position of the Hegelian Trinity—Its relation to self-consciousness—Attempt to simplify the subject by analogy—Transference of the human idea to the divine nature—Necessity for a Trinity in the divine nature—Defence of the evangelical interpretation of the Hegelian Theology—Distinction between the Hegelian Trinity as it is in eternity and as it appears in time, . . . 91

CHAPTER IX.

EVOLUTION OF THE HEGELIAN TRINITY IN TIME.

Necessity for a creation—Inadequacy of the first creation to embody the Divine Spirit—Development of the divine life in nature from inertness to dormancy, and thence to intelligence—Struggle in the human spirit between nature and will—Restoration of nature and humanity in the Son of man, ... 102

CHAPTER X.

EVOLUTION OF THE HEGELIAN TRINITY IN THE HISTORY OF THE CHURCH.

Life of the risen Christ manifested in the Church—Three stages of Church development—External period—Reaction from the external period in the Reformation—Abuse of the Reformation principle—Attempt of the Hegelian Theology to find a balance between the external and internal spirit, . 111

CHAPTER XI.

THE RIGHT AND THE LEFT.

Explanation of the difference between these interpretations—Examination of the principle on which the Left Hegelianism reposes—Cause of the prevalence of this theology—Enumeration of the different attempts to mediate between the Right and the Left, ... 120

CHAPTER XII.

MYTHICAL THEORY OF STRAUSS.

David Strauss—External and internal side of his system—Sense in which he uses the word mythical—His defence of his position as a Christian minister—Comparison of his scepticism with that of the Deists of the 18th century—Difficulties which his own theory has to encounter, . . . 134

CHAPTER XIII.

BREAKING UP OF THE MYTHICAL THEORY—SCHOOL OF TÜBINGEN.

Bruno Bauer—F. C. Baur of Tübingen—Baur's statement of the facts of gospel history—His theory to account for these facts—Examination of the sense in which Baur's theory is a development of the mythical one—Examination of the sense in which it is a revolt from the mythical theory—Baur's unconscious concession to Christianity, and examination of the inference we derive from it, ... 146

CHAPTER XIV.

BREAKING UP OF THE MYTHICAL THEORY CONTINUED—SIGNS OF A RETURN TO THE OLD RATIONALISM.

Revival of Rationalism—Comparison of Renan and Schenkel—Mixture of Mythicism with their Rationalism—Theological position of Ewald—Want of unanimity amongst the opponents of historical Christianity, ... 156

CHAPTER XV.

'THE OLD FAITH AND THE NEW.'

Abandonment of mythical theory by Strauss in his last work—His four questions—Examination of his definition of religion, of his objection to a Personal God, and of his opposition to the doctrine of Immortality—Final goal of negative criticism—Examination of the sense in which it may not be called materialistic—Its present influence in Germany—Entire one-sidedness of this latest philosophy, . . . 164

CHAPTER XVI.

PARALLEL BETWEEN THE HISTORY OF ENGLISH AND GERMAN THEOLOGY.

Advantage of a retrospective view—Existence of a historical parallel between English and German theology—Medieval reactions against the hierarchy—Mutual and independent movement at the Reformation—Simultaneous declension after the Reformation—Rise and progress of Rationalism in both countries—Methodism and Pietism; cause of their failure—Rationalism foiled by her own weapons—Comparison of Kant and Hume—Condition of English and German theology after the destruction of Rationalism, and present relation of physical science in England to speculative thought in Germany, ... 172

SUPPLEMENTARY NOTES, ... 183

INDEX, ... 217

AIDS TO
THE STUDY OF GERMAN THEOLOGY.

INTRODUCTION.

WE offer this work to the student as an attempt to supply a desideratum. The exposition of German theology is as yet an almost untrodden field. Indeed, it is a fact which cannot be denied, that the ecclesiastical history of this century has yet to be written. Neander, unquestionably the prince of Church historians, was arrested by the hand of death ere his work had well entered the Middle Ages. Mosheim, who is little conversant with theories, and not very reliable in facts, belongs to an age which even from our sympathies has passed away. Gieseler did not extend his labours further than 1780. Hagenbach's *History of Doctrines* is a mere fragmentary sketch, rather intended as an index to reading than in itself a source of information. Dorner's *Protestant Theology* opens up a broad ocean, but as it nears our own days it narrows into a tiny stream. And even although these materials were more complete than they are, there would still remain an impassable barrier to the student at the entrance of his course. It has long since been discovered that the views of a German author cannot be unveiled by the mere translation of German words into an English vocabulary. The views of a Frenchman can be made manifest in this way; but the reason is plain. There is a certain analogy between the French and English mind; in both, the empirical predominates over the ideal; with both, the testimony of sense is received as the surest starting-point. But the German is radically different; his thoughts run not so much from without to within as from within to without. It is vain to say that this manifestation of the German mind is an ephemeral growth, an accident of the present century; to speak thus is to betray an ignorance of all history. It is a notorious fact, that while the greater part of Europe was in bondage to the sensualism and legalism of the Roman hierarchy, the Teutonic intellect had already begun to exhibit the germs of that speculative spirit which in modern times has burst into flower. It was here that originated that wonderful anticipation of the Protestant reaction which has been stamped, though we think erroneously, with the name of Mysticism; for Mysticism is in truth the only exhibition of practical Christianity which we meet with in the Middle Ages.[1] It withdrew itself, indeed, from the things of sense; but why so? because these things of sense had been invested with a mystical and magical bias. The Romanists were the true mystics, and they who bear that name were really the precursors

[1] See supplementary note, page 183.

Introduction. 3

of a practical faith. The so-called mystics, Tauler, Ruysbroeck, Staupitz, Wesel, and such as they, were men who saw in God something more than could be represented in a pageant or imaged in a crucifix, who sought a deeper life than that of sensuous worship, and who found a benign joy in sources which the world had not fathomed. By the age in which they lived they were not only misunderstood and unappreciated, but were even objects of dislike and aversion. Men are ever suspicious of that which they cannot understand, and then, as now, the thoughts of the German mind needed translation. It was the ideas and not the words which required to be interpreted. In that age there might be said to be one language. Nearly all literary men wrote in Latin, and therefore in this respect the ancient student had facilities over the modern one. Nevertheless, this uniformity of language did not prevent the German mystics from constituting a peculiar class, distinct from all beside. They stood as much apart from the ordinary thought of their era as if they had been shut out from all means of verbal communication with the men of their age. It was the different standpoint of their thought which made them peculiar; and in order to remove their isolation, the world must be made to think along with them. The so-called transcendentalism of Germany, therefore, is no accidental manifestation or temporary ebullition; it is only the culminating stage of that which has always been its natural characteristic. And if even during the Medieval Age the use of a common language did not render the mind of Germany accessible to the mass of mankind, we need not be surprised to find that the modern student has to experience a still more arduous task in translating the ideas of that nation both into language and into thought. It will be the object of these pages to furnish the student with a key to thought-translation. Their design is neither apologetic nor critical, but simply interpretative. They aim at the transmutation of German ideas into the garb of English thought; until that is done, any verbal translation must leave the matter where it found it. We must endeavour to see wherein consists that charge of vagueness and obscurity which has been constantly preferred against the German theology. For ourselves, we are persuaded that the vagueness lies not in the theology itself, but in the fact that it abounds in expressions which do not admit of rendering into any language, and that the only way to remove that vagueness is to disregard the word and describe the thing. We shall therefore discard all technical language. We shall never speak of an Ego or a non-Ego when we can describe our meaning by any English parallel. We shall avoid as much as possible those ungainly terms of nomenclature which, like the cherubim and the flaming sword, stand on the threshold of the subject, and drive away him who would enter in. We shall try to approach this study with that simplicity of statement and that clearness of illustration which alone can render it intelligible; and if in any measure, however small, we shall succeed in smoothing the path of the

Introduction. 5

inquirer, the object of these labours shall have been amply attained.

We have taken as our starting-point the theology of Kant. Indeed German theology, in its most recent aspect, may be said to begin with him. It is with Kant that, for the first time, the German mind completely emancipates itself from contact with foreign elements, and stands out in absolute, unalloyed originality. Before this period the theology of Germany, while it had ever a certain freshness and independence, was yet to some extent incorporated both with French and English thought. Perhaps the earliest of her systematic philosophers was Leibnitz; yet it is undeniable that Leibnitz derived his impulse, and in great measure shaped his theory, from the system of Des Cartes in France. The philosophy of Leibnitz is much more French than German; and it is not surprising that a system which professed to find the reason of all things, should in its last resort, at the close of the eighteenth century, have met hand in hand with the illuminism of Diderot and D'Alembert. Leibnitz is the father of German Rationalism; but Leibnitz was the pupil of Des Cartes, and therefore the Rationalism which he bequeathed to his country was something transplanted, not indigenous. The expression 'German Rationalism' has become almost proverbial, but in truth Rationalism never found in Germany anything but a foreign soil; it was always in direct antagonism to the spirit of the nation. As in the Medieval period we see the Teutonic mind opposing itself to Romanism, as something foreign to its nature, so during the greater part of last century we find it struggling, in a thousand reactions, to liberate itself from that Rationalism which was equally foreign to its spirit. To the mind of Germany, Romanism and Rationalism have been equally obnoxious, and for precisely the same reason; both have sought to rest truth upon an authority inferior to itself—Romanism on tradition, Rationalism on apologetic evidences. Indeed, neither of these systems would have existed for an hour if they had not proclaimed themselves the allies of Christianity. For it is to be observed, that in Germany Rationalism did not, any more than Romanism, begin by antagonism to the revealed word. On the contrary, she announced herself as the handmaid of Christian truth; she professed to surround revelation with a bulwark which all the efforts of scepticism and all the attacks of infidelity would never be able to destroy; she began by accepting the entire testimony of Scripture in all the integrity of its doctrines and precepts, and only requested permission to render its authority more secure by establishing on grounds of reason what had been received by the light of faith. It was a dangerous request—a demand which carried in its very bosom the nightshade of destruction. For even in this stage of comparative purity, Rationalism had already manifested the beginnings of that pride which ultimately produced not her own fall only, but the complete annihilation of all belief whatsoever. To say that human reason is adequate to explain revelation when-

Introduction.

ever we have received it, is only one step removed from saying that human reason is adequate in itself to unveil the mysteries of God. Nor was that step long in being taken. Rationalism soon found that those doctrines which lie at the heart of Christianity were incapable of logical demonstration. When she made this discovery there were two courses open to her. She might have abandoned the field as untenable: this would have been honest, for she had already received Scripture as her authority. But pride forbade such a sacrifice. It was hard to give up such a beautifully concocted scheme, especially when another course remained. Why should Rationalism be all in the wrong, and Scripture all in the right? Might not this antiquated book contain errors of statement, accommodations to the age in which it was written, mythical representations whose origin was lost in the mist of distance? Here was the second road open to Rationalism, and she chose it. The doctrine of the Trinity could not be measured by human reason. So much the worse for the doctrine of the Trinity; it must henceforth be eliminated from the sacred record. With this doctrine went another,—that of Christ's eternal Sonship. Toellner denied His active obedience, and affirmed His subordination. Dœderlin adopted Arianism, and declared that His work was not to satisfy God, but to soothe man. Eberhard, Steinbart, and Löffler rejected even the semblance of satisfaction, and reduced the mission of Christ to that of a gifted human teacher. The Lutheran Church itself unconsciously hastened the era of theological destruction. We find such men as Less, Spalding, Miller, Jerusalem, and Nosselt, who were truly the representatives of their age, boldly advocating the limitation of pulpit discourses to the teaching of practical morality, and the exclusion of all doctrinal questions as belonging to the sphere of mystery. If the orthodox Church of Germany could thus speak, we cannot wonder that Rationalism should gather strength by her concessions. The Church had enjoined that the doctrines of Scripture should, as much as possible, be left alone; in doing so she left open for Rationalism only one remaining step to complete the reign of unbelief, and that was to assert that there were no doctrines in Scripture at all. That step was taken by Semler. With him falls to the ground the last trace of dogmatic Christianity. He proclaims that the religion of Christ had been all along mistaken by the world. Christ came not to inculcate truth, but to point out the road to virtue. His mission was not one of revelation, but one of advice. The substance of His teaching is better seen in the Sermon on the Mount than in the mystical discourse of the fourth Gospel. These are foreign accretions, the additions of a later age, the philosophizings of some Hellenist who wanted to make Christianity an echo of his own Platonism; but the primitive form of Christ's religion must be sought in the words of the holy Mount, and the utterances by the lake of Gennesaret. Such was the creed of Semler. In relation to theology Rationalism could go no further; she had now done her worst. But although, so far as theology was concerned, Rationalism had exhausted her weapons of destruction, she had still another world to conquer; that world was the very morality which Semler proposed to substitute for Christian doctrine, for it is a great mistake to suppose that the absolute domain of reason can destroy Christianity and yet leave morality untouched. If everything must be brought within the pale of reason, so must right and wrong. When we pronounce an action good or bad, we do not feel ourselves bound to assign any reason for our judgment beyond the testimony of conscience. But if we start with the principle of Rationalism, that nothing exists which has not its ground in human reason, then morality becomes utility,—the right is the useful, the wrong is the injurious; virtue is only good because it leads to happiness, vice is only bad because it conducts to misery. This is the doctrine which the student will meet under the name of Eudæmonism; it is the doctrine of Paley, of Stuart Mill, of the large majority of scientific men in our own country at the present day, and it was the universal doctrine of German Rationalists in the eighteenth century. It is the legitimate outcome of the Rationalistic premises, and therefore this system has at least the merit of self-consistency.

Such was the condition of Germany when Kant appeared upon the scene. The empire of reason had extended itself alike to heaven and earth, had reduced all revelation to the realm of nature, and all morality to the one virtue of worldly prudence. But the extremity of all things is the beginning of their change. The time was coming when, over the length and breadth of the German nation, the mandate was to go forth, 'Let there be light;' but before that voice could be heard, it was necessary that another voice should precede it, 'Let there be chaos.' There must be destruction ere there could be reconstruction; the systems of human pride must be rent into fragments, the vaunting claims of reason must be levelled with the dust. Man must be taught, first of all, his own insignificance as a thinker; he must be made to feel that, so far from having grasped the mysteries of the universe, he cannot even attain to one absolute fact of knowledge. That was the gospel which God had first to proclaim to Germany,—the gospel of human helplessness, almost of human despair. The hour had come for its proclamation, and the man had come with the hour. That man was Kant. He came with a mission almost apostolic. He was commissioned to be the apostle of destruction; he was sent to be a son of thunder, to call down the fire from heaven. His essential work was to destroy, to prove that all the efforts of reason to explain the mystery of life had been vanity of vanities. To that mission he was faithful to the end; he reduced the proud trophies of the human intellect to a heap of ruins. We will not deny that in this work of destruction he rooted up with the tares some portions of the precious wheat; it is not possible to perform any great work without inflicting some individual injuries. But conceding all this, it still remains a fact indisputable, that the philosophy of Kant, or rather his destruction of all absolute philosophy, was God's greatest gift to the Germany of the eighteenth century. It purified the atmosphere from these mists which were but the exhalations of the breath of man, and which man had mistaken for the shadow of Deity; and if in clearing them away it left a temporary vacuum, a world without form and void, yet by that very act it prepared the way for the inauguration of a brighter era, the advent of that hour when man would see by the light of God.

NOTE.—The student will understand that we speak of Kant as a destroyer in a purely theological sense. As a metaphysician he was a great reconstructor, and succeeded in reducing to unity the existing laws of the human mind; but he denied that these laws, or this unity, could be known to have any absolute existence outside the human consciousness.

CHAPTER I.

THE NATURAL THEOLOGY OF KANT.

REASON, as we have seen, had claimed a perfect understanding of divine mysteries. Kant undertook to prove that, so far from grasping the mysteries of God, reason could not even establish His being. We proceed to exhibit in detail that process of refutation by which Kant overthrew on the very threshold the claims of Rationalism. In this and succeeding chapters we shall often find it convenient to exhibit the system of a writer as if it were unfolded by himself. Let the student understand that, in these cases, we shall not quote the words of the author, but merely paraphrase them—make him speak as we would imagine him to have spoken had he been an Englishman; in this way we shall best succeed in making our subject intelligible.

The student is probably aware that reason has devised three great arguments to establish the being of a God; these are called respectively the Ontological, the Cosmological, and the Teleological. Kant attacks them one by one; and we shall exhibit his reasoning in three corresponding sections.

Sect. I.—Ontological Argument.

The ontological argument has various forms, which, as we are not discussing theology in general, we are not required to enumerate. It has, however, one aspect common to all the forms, in which it may be represented thus: 'We have an idea of God.' That idea does not come from nature, because nature cannot exhibit anything but the change of phenomena. It cannot come from our own souls, because we, who are naturally so imperfect, could not possibly of ourselves create the idea of a perfect being. There is only one remaining source from which it can come, and that is God Himself. Such is the ontological argument; it infers the existence of God in the universe from the idea of Him in our own minds. Kant says that this reasoning is not valid. What right have we to conclude that, because we have the idea of a perfect being, that idea must have an objective or outward existence? Have we not many conceptions within our minds which we cannot refer to any corresponding object in the outer world? The contact with a warm substance produces the sensation of heat; we may believe that this sensation is caused by some outward object, but have we any right to affirm that the object without has a resemblance to the sensation within? On the contrary, we know that it can have no such resemblance, any more than the cheerfulness awakened by the sunbeams can resemble the sunbeams which awakened it. Such is, in spirit, the reasoning of

Kant. We think it valid, so far as it goes. We cannot prove the existence of an outward God from the mere idea of Him; but the question remains, Why should we seek a God out of the universe of thought? Such a God is the God of the deist, not of the Christian. Why did not Kant maintain that the idea of God is God Himself in the soul? Such a statement would at once have been a refutation of Rationalism and a corroboration of Scripture, for it is the express doctrine of Scripture that it is only in God's light that we see light.

But Kant left it for Hegel to say that. Kant was only a destroyer; and when the destruction was completed, his proper work was done. Yet let us do him justice. The demolition of the ontological argument, while it is powerless against the God of Christianity, is omnipotent against the God of Rationalism. The Supreme Being whom the Rationalist professes to worship is a God dwelling afar off, outside of thought, beyond the universe, removed by an infinite distance both of space and time from all His works,—a Being who, at some remote era of antiquity, did indeed create the heavens and the earth, or at least fashioned the germs from which they sprang, but who has since vacated the reins of empire to the vicegerency of law, and, for all that we can know to the contrary, may have passed out of being altogether. Such is the God of Rationalism. Surely Kant did not overstep the mark when he said that such a Being was incapable either of being proved or known; surely he did not say too much

Cosmological Argument.

when he characterized His existence as an idea, and nothing more. His penetrating intellect discerned that Deism had set up as an object of worship the offspring of its own imagination, and deified as an idol the image of human imperfection; and if he succeeded in dashing that idol to the ground, he has left a real and permanent contribution to the researches of theology and the advance of religious thought.

Sect. II.—Cosmological Argument.

The second argument by which reason has sought to establish the being of a God is called the cosmological, and is briefly the following syllogism: 'Every effect must have a cause; the universe is an effect, therefore the universe must have a cause.' Kant attacked this argument also, and in a totally different manner from that in which he had assailed the previous one. His reasoning amounts to this: It is equally impossible to conceive this world as an independent cause, or as the effect of an independent cause. On the one hand, we cannot imagine this world to have had no beginning, for in that case we would be obliged to suppose an infinite series of individuals going back into the past eternity; and as none of these individuals is self-supporting, we would never be able to account for this unbeginning life. On the other hand, it is equally difficult to imagine this world as the effect of an eternal First Cause, because the very expression 'eternal First Cause' seems to contradict the cosmological argument. That argument holds that every effect must have a cause; but an eternal First Cause is something which exists without any reason—which is at once its own cause and its own effect; it is, therefore, says Kant, equally impossible to conceive either that this world had or that it had not a beginning. Here, again, the argument is omnipotent against Rationalism, but powerless against Christianity, for in Christianity God is as much the First Cause now as He was at the beginning; preservation is an eternal creation. In Christianity, the beginning or the non-beginning of the world has nothing to do with the necessity for a God; God would be equally necessary though we had no record of a creation. Suppose we grant it, for the sake of argument, that this world might be eternal, what would be the consequence? Would the legitimate conclusion be Atheism? Assuredly not. We need a God to account for every present moment. We feel and see, that however eternal this world might be, it could never be anything but a contingent world, vanishing, changing, passing away; and if it could be proved that there never was a time when it was called into existence by the word of God, it would still require that word to explain the upholding of its existence; it could only be conceived as eternal if recognised as an eternal emanation of God. The cosmological argument, therefore, while it is broken in the hands of the Rationalists, stands steadfast in the grasp of Christianity, for here there is only one everlasting Cause—

a perpetual Creator, in whose light alone all things appear, and in whose breath alone all things live. Here we stand every moment in the first morning of creation, and listen to the omnipotent fiat, 'Let there be light.' The creative power of God is not an attribute in search of which we must travel back over centuries and ages, for it is present with us every day and hour, and what we call the law of nature is the miracle of life.

SECT. III.—TELEOLOGICAL ARGUMENT.

The teleological argument is that which in our country is popularly known as the argument from design, and may be stated thus: Design implies a designer; the universe exhibits design, and therefore the universe implies a designer. Even Kant admits that this argument is the best of the three, and says that it should never be mentioned without respect. Nevertheless, he considers it invalid, and for this reason, that it will not yield God, but only a being great enough to make the universe. The most which the argument from design can yield is an architect of power so stupendous that he could create the whole mechanism of this world and of all worlds; but this, says Kant, is a finite power after all; we do not suppose the world to be infinite, and therefore its designer need not be infinite. Now here once more we have an argument omnipotent against Rationalism, because with Rationalism this world is indeed a finite thing; it is far removed from God. But it is not so with Christianity; here God is in His works, and therefore there is a sense in which this world is not finite, but infinite. That this world has an infinite side may be seen from the most commonplace illustrations. For example, a pebble on the beach is in one sense a finite thing, but in another sense it is infinite; it is infinitely divisible; you might break it up into an endless number of parts. We cannot conceive that any object in the universe could by division be reduced to vacuum. We can imagine that it could be rendered so small that its perception might require the aid of the microscope, or even to such an extent that the microscope itself would be powerless to detect it; but even in these cases we could never bring ourselves to believe that the object itself had been annihilated. It is thus that, in the most everyday appearances, we are confronted by the infinitude of this world, that in every finite phenomenon we discover an infinite possibility. It was this truth which in later years was so grandly observed and illustrated by the master mind of Hegel. It was he who recognised beneath all temporal appearances something which the temporal could not explain, which pointed onwards for its consummation, and which found its completeness only in the thought of the divine. With him this universe bursts out, as it were, into fresh glory, for it reveals itself in an aspect undiscovered before,—one half the product of earth, and the other the shadow of heaven; one pointing to the limited, the finite, the mutable, and

Teleological Argument.

the other to the universal, the infinite, the eternal; one bearing the impress of man, and the other the adumbration of God. Kant destroyed the temple; Hegel from its ruins built it up anew.

We have now, in these foregoing sections, tried to exhibit the effect of Kant's philosophy on the current systems of Rationalism. We have said that he was essentially a destroyer; that when the destruction was complete his proper work was done; and that it was reserved for Hegel to build up what he had destroyed. It must not be thought, however, that Kant arrogated to himself no higher distinction than that of an iconoclast; he, too, professed to reconstruct that which he had broken down. In this attempt at reconstruction we believe he transcended his mission, and are convinced that he signally failed; it is only fair, however, to examine his method. Kant had succeeded in demolishing the three arguments for the God of Rationalism; but having chased the enemy from the field, he is unwilling to leave it unoccupied. He professes to re-establish the demonstration of God's existence upon a new and higher basis—that of our moral nature. He says: 'We feel within our finite being something which seems to exist in spite of it; it is the sense of freedom.' 'There is something within us which tells us we are free.' 'Conscience says you ought, therefore you can.' 'The sense of responsibility necessitates our freedom.' 'Nevertheless, reason says we are not free, and experience confirms reason.' 'Our will is in a state of slavery; the evil which we would not, that we do; the good which we would, that we do not.'

How is this discrepancy to be reconciled? Can we at one moment be both free and slaves? Can the testimony of conscience contradict the testimony of fact? Kant professes to solve the contradiction by the doctrines of God and Immortality. Conscience says, 'You ought, therefore you can.' The chains of nature say, 'You are enslaved, therefore you cannot.' The chains of nature hold possession of the present, but the voice of conscience is the harbinger of the future. It tells us that we have on earth an unsupplied faculty of our nature, a sense without an object, an instinct which has found no temporal use or end; and therefore it points onward to the existence of a life beyond the temporal, and to the being of One in whose light the soul shall find its perfect freedom: the sense of human responsibility is the herald of God and immortality.

Such is Kant's argument for a natural theology. The thought is beautiful, sublime, suggestive, and spiritually true. But a thing may be spiritually true, and yet not a valid argument; argument belongs to the intellect, spiritual truth to the heart. Kant advances his thought as an argument, and therefore in this light it must be tested. And in this light we think it cannot stand. Might not the Rationalist throw back at Kant those very weapons which he had flung at himself? Might he not, with justice, retort upon him: 'You say that my notion of God may be a mere idea; granted, but so may your notion of freedom. How do you know that this grand sense of human responsibility is not a figment of your own brain, an imagination, a dream? You may appeal for its truth to the feelings of the heart, but in the very act of doing so you abandon your ground; feeling is not argument, and you have professed by argument to build up what you have destroyed. Prove that your reasoning is more valid than mine. Prove that the idea of freedom is more real than that of cause and effect, which latter you pronounce a mere form of human thought. When you have done so, you may claim the merit of reconstruction; until then, you must abide as a sceptic and destroyer.' Such we conceive to be the terms in which the Rationalist might retort on Kant, and we cannot say that such an answer would be either unjust or unreasonable. Conscience does not testify to responsibility more clearly than intellect does to the necessity of a first cause and the principle of design in nature; if the latter be merely forms of thought, there is no reason why the former should be anything more. We are, therefore, reluctantly obliged to leave Kant in the position of a destroyer, and to regard his work as really accomplished when he broke the idols of Rationalism, and shattered the arguments in favour of an unknown God. Ere we part with him, however, we must take a glance at that method of interpretation by which he sought to attach his new system of natural theology to the facts and events of the Scripture narrative; and in the study of this we shall yet more amply see how he realized his character of a destroyer, in obliterating from the sacred records all historical significance. We shall therefore, in the next chapter, give a thought-translation of Kant's system of doctrines—that is to say, we shall allow him to speak for himself, by rendering into English, not his language, indeed, but his ideas. The German spirit being thus clothed in the English form, the student will be able to arrive at a definite understanding of the Kantian Theology, and may afterwards, at a more advanced stage, verify the matter for himself.

CHAPTER II.

KANT'S INTERPRETATION OF THE FACTS OF SCRIPTURE.

I.—THE FALL.

HUMANITY may be conceived as originally existing in subjection to the law of God; for true freedom consists not in liberty of choice between good and evil, but in the voluntary obedience of our spirits to the principle of virtue as a necessity of their nature. The power of choice, so far from being a mark of freedom, was in truth the beginning of slavery, for it indicated that the soul was no longer bound by virtue as a necessary part of its being. Whenever we begin to choose between right and wrong, we place right and wrong upon an equality. Hence the soul, when it placed before itself the alternatives of good and evil, was already fallen; the evil lay in the choice. The alternatives before the soul were the moral law and self-love, and it chose the latter. This was not wonderful, seeing that self-love had already begun in the very act of choice. And so man fell; and his fall consisted in this, that his universal will became an individual wish. He no longer desired the good of all, but the good of himself; he no longer sought for the happiness of mankind, but for the gratification of his own passions; he no longer felt himself to be Man, but only a particular man, a unit whose interests must be attended to. Hence the essence of the Fall was selfishness; it was both its cause and its effect. It was self-love which induced man to desire independence of God, and his punishment was just the gratification of that desire; he was left alone to seek his own good after his own manner.

REMARK. — The student will here observe that thus far the view of Kant is not only scriptural but Calvinistic; indeed, Kant's account of the Fall bears a strong analogy to that of Augustine. In what follows, however, we observe the divergence from Scripture. In relation to the Fall, Kant was under less temptation to diverge, because this doctrine belongs as much to reason as to revelation, and seems even to prevail in the Platonic philosophy.[1]

II.—POSSIBILITY OF REDEMPTION.

We have no right to say that the fall of man was in its nature irremediable. The will was enslaved, indeed, yet as a faculty it was not impaired. To pinion a man's arms is to deprive him of power; yet the power remains theoretically in the arms, though incapable of practical exercise. There was nothing, therefore, in the nature of things to prevent the will from coming back again to its first state. By an in-

[1] See supplementary note, page 185.

comprehensible act it fell; by an incomprehensible act it may rise again. If it be said, how can a nature utterly depraved return by its own strength into purity? may it not be answered with great force and truth, how could a nature perfectly pure fall down by its own strength into a state of depravity? It is surely as easy to imagine a self-regeneration from sin to holiness, as it is to account for the undoubted fact of a self-degradation from holiness to sin.

III.—CONDITIONS NECESSARY TO REDEMPTION.

Man, then, may redeem himself; but he cannot do so without certain conditions. There are three necessary conditions to redemption. In the first place, the individual man must form to himself a lofty ideal—the ideal of a perfect moral life. Whenever a man has set up in his mind such a standard of excellence, his redemption is already begun. True, his actions may not yet correspond to his aspirations: the opinions are the angel part of us, and it is no uncommon thing to find lofty views conjoined with bad practice. Nevertheless, the setting up of a high standard is the birth of the new man within us; and if our actions do not at once come into harmony with our thoughts, it is only because the new man must bear the sins of the old, even while it prophesies their removal. This is the true meaning of vicarious satisfaction.

The second condition necessary to redemption is a historical Christ—that is to say, an actual living being in some respect corresponding to our idea of the perfect man. The idea must attach itself to something in the outer world. It is not necessary, indeed, that the historical Christ should be all that is said of him. He need not be divine in any supernatural sense, he need not be born in any peculiar way, nor need his life be marked by absolute sinlessness; all that is wanted is, that he should furnish the occasion for awakening our idea of what a perfect man should be. Above all, the historical Christ must not be regarded as an authority, for authority is destructive to morality; his value must lie, and lie exclusively, in this, that he has suggested to humanity the thought of a perfect ideal. Henceforth the ideal Christ becomes our sole guide; the historical was merely the ladder by which we climbed to it, and having reached the height, we are entitled to throw the ladder down.[1]

But there remains one other condition necessary to redemption, and that is an ethical community or ideal Church. The essence of sin is selfishness, and the essence of selfishness is individualism; that is to say, the forgetfulness that we are something more than mere units—that we have a common life, a brotherhood, a kindred humanity which makes us all one. Now there can be no redemption until this is realized. We must come to feel that our truest interests are not our interests as individuals, but our interests as a united family. We must rise into the conviction that we have a higher life than that personal existence

[1] See supplementary note, p. 188.

which strives and frets upon the surface of the wave; that there is beneath our personality something which we share with all personalities,—an electric chord which binds together the hearts and thoughts of all living men, and which links in one indissoluble bond the whole race of Man. The recognition of this truth is the discovery that we are members of a great invisible Church, that we are united by the profession of one common morality, and that our most sacred instincts are ever to be found in that sense of union to which we give the name of humanity.

REMARK.—The student will here observe that redemption, with Kant, has no reference whatever to God; it is simply personal reformation, and therefore in his system it has nothing to do with theology at all. The reason of this is plain; Kant does not admit the possibility of a theology, as will appear in the following sections.

IV.—NATURE OF GOD.

The nature of God is unknowable. We have, indeed, an idea of the Absolute, but we have no right to say that our idea represents the truth; it is at best only a generalization of our human knowledge, a combination of our experiences into one grand whole. That there is anything corresponding to our idea in the outer universe is a mere dictum of faith, not an inference of philosophy.

V.—THE TRINITY.

We may think of God in a threefold capacity: 1*st*, as the Creator; 2*d*, as the Preserver and Governor; and 3*d*, as the Administrator of Moral Law. We may think of Him so, though we must not suppose that He is so. God in Himself is unknowable, and we can do nothing more than classify the different impressions which His works produce upon us. In this sense, and in this alone, we may discover something which may be called a Trinity; and we are entitled to use the name, provided always we understand that the distinctions are not in God, but in our own imperfect thoughts. If we were perfect, we would be able to contemplate God as a grand unity, but because our faculties are limited, we are obliged to divide His works into departments, just as we separate human knowledge into various branches of art and science. These are the resorts of man's weakness.

VI.—REVELATION.

An outward revelation is a contradiction in terms. God, not being material, cannot reveal Himself in matter, or through the senses. As little can He speak to us through the powers of reason, for the materials of reason are derived solely from the external world, and therefore the thoughts of reason must be on a level with their source. There is, however, one part of our nature independent of sensuous forms, independent of space and time, the same yesterday and to-day and for ever: it is the voice of conscience—that which says, 'You ought, therefore you can.'

It speaks with a power absolutely unqualified, and therefore it is the only possible meeting-place between the finite and Infinite. It is only here that revelation can have any force. If God would reveal Himself to man, it must be through his moral nature, and the truths which revelation teaches must be moral truths. These ideas communicated by revelation are three in number: Liberty, God, and Immortality. We learn the liberty of the will from the dictum of conscience. You ought, therefore you can; it is involved in the sense of responsibility. We learn God and immortality from the fact that in this world we have no actual liberty; and as we have the idea of responsible freedom, that idea points onwards, to find its solution in a higher life.

VII.—PERSON OF CHRIST.

This doctrine has been already virtually included in the conditions necessary to redemption. In speaking of these, it was affirmed that the historical Christ derives his whole significance from being the originator of a grand thought, the ideal of a perfect man; and that when our minds have formed this ideal, the historical Christ may cease to be an object of veneration. The true Christ, therefore, is the inward idea, the conception of a perfect man. It may be said metaphorically to come down from heaven, because it is a thought which never could have proceeded from an earthly nature. It exists in man rather as a guest than as a natural inmate, and is engaged in constant struggle with the lower parts of our being; the ideal points upward, while the old man grovels on the earth. The flesh lusteth against the spirit, and the spirit against the flesh: what is that but the new man bearing the sins of the old? It is the same thing as the Latin poet has expressed in the words, 'I see and approve better things; I follow worse.' The seeing and approving of the better things is just the inward Christ,—the aspiration after a perfect life, the thought of ideal purity. The following of the worse things is just the crucifixion of that Christ, the betrayal of our convictions, the mocking of our loftiest nature, the preference of the natural Barabbas to the heavenly King who is sent to bear witness to the truth. Yet even in the act of crucifixion this inward Christ is the forerunner of a resurrection. An ideal of purity, even where it is not exhibited in practice, is yet prophetic of a coming regeneration, and tells of a time when the old man in turn shall be crucified by the new, and when the kingdoms of this world shall become the kingdoms of our God and of His Christ.

Summing up of Results.

Such is a brief, yet, we think, an exhaustive statement of the Kantian philosophy in so far as it refers to religion. It would be unjust to deny that it has great and lasting merits, and has left, in some respects a claim to the gratitude of all. It has destroyed the pride of human reason, by demonstrating its impotence to unravel things divine. It has destroyed the belief in Eudæmonism—that is to say, the belief that goodness is nothing but utility, for it has given such a prominence· to the authority of conscience, that morality must henceforth shine by its own light. It has even indirectly borne a testimony to the truth of Christianity, for it has shown that the ideas of Christianity are eternal ideas, that the historical framework is the expression and embodiment of the deepest instincts of the human heart. These are the merits of Kant; let us confess them candidly and fearlessly, and all the more so because, when we have said this, we have summed up all that can be said in favour of his system. As an attempt to build up what he had successfully destroyed, the system of Kant was an utter, an egregious failure. So far from establishing a theology, it resulted in the negation of all theology. In the hands of Kant, the doctrines of Christianity are merely the unaided gropings of an unsatisfied moral nature; gropings which may be true, or which may be false, but whose truth or falsity is incapable of being verified. The facts of Christianity are with him not so much matters of unbelief as matters of indifference, the mere symbols in which the inward idea has clothed itself in order to express itself to the world. Hence all history becomes a dream, or at least a dream would serve as well; if the mind wants nothing but a poetical image, it can matter little whether that image be real or fictitious. In Kant we see the beginning of that rupture with all external things which found its terrible completion in the atheism of his disciple Fichte. His work was done when he had destroyed the false; it was reserved for others to build up the true. Kant razed to earth those walls of Rationalism which had sought to enclose the light of heaven, but it was not given to him to rear a temple in their room; he extinguished the artificial lamp of reason, but he could not say to the natural darkness, 'Let there be light.'

CHAPTER III.

TRANSITION TO SCHLEIERMACHER.

WE have seen that Kant left everything in a state of negation. In sinking the ship of Rationalism, he destroyed the anchor along with it, and the German world, in losing its false belief, had lost all belief whatsoever. Now in times of negation there always appear two opposing tendencies. One section of mankind abandons itself to universal scepticism, and considers the only certainty in human knowledge to be the impossibility of knowing anything. There are others, again, who adopt the opposite extreme. Finding that the human intellect is powerless to solve the problem, they repudiate, indeed, the claim of intellect to touch divine things, but do not on that account reject divine things themselves. They set up another standard, blind faith—faith not founded on reason, but on some authority or testimony outside of reason, and independent of it. These are the two tendencies which inevitably spring up from a state of negation; and in that religious world of Germany which had been permeated by the Kantian philosophy, we find that both of them simultaneously arise. Hence Kant may be regarded as the father of two schools,—

the one tending to implicit faith, the other to absolute unbelief. From him there branched forth two straight lines, which never could meet, although they had a common origin. It shall be our object in succession to trace each of these lines, for to one or other of these all the different phases of German theology may be referred. And we propose to begin with that tendency which endeavoured to escape from negation by substituting for the limitations of intellect the authority of faith. This tendency assumed two forms. Some rested their faith on the testimony of an infallible hierarchy. Such was Schlegel, who, oppressed with the Kantian scepticism, found no repose until he had joined the membership of the Roman Catholic Church. In so doing, he, and such as he, passed outside the range of German theology, and have no further concern with the subject of this inquiry. But it is to the other form of this tendency that we must specially address ourselves, because it marks the transition to one who has exercised a gigantic influence not only over the theology of Germany, but over the religious life of modern Europe itself—we mean Schleiermacher. The form of thought here alluded to is the identification of religious belief with religious feeling. It tells us to disregard the difficulties created by reason, nay, even to ignore all rational and dogmatic views of Christianity, and to confine our attention exclusively to the perceptions of the heart—to make these at once the object and the ground of our faith. The immediate transition to this school is, indeed, not Schleier-

Transition to Schleiermacher. 35

macher, but Jacobi. Jacobi defines religion to be faith founded on feeling of the reality of the ideal. Nevertheless, with Jacobi, the feeling of religion was rather poetical than vital; it belonged more to the imagination than to the heart. It was the feeling with which a poet contemplates the beauties of nature, or with which an artist surveys the picture on his canvas. With Jacobi it was a small thing whether or not the feeling were true; the value lay in the belief, and not in the thing believed. Religion was to him a grand elevation of sentiment, a lever which lifted the mind into an atmosphere of pure ethereal contemplation, and which raised it for a time above the petty cares of life. This was, after all, but the sensation awakened by the reading of a beautiful romance; it indicated a fine æsthetic taste, but was no proof whatever of vital piety. Nor is De Wette in this respect much superior to Jacobi, at least in his earlier writings. It is pleasing, no doubt, to observe that, as De Wette advanced in years, he approached nearer and nearer to belief in historical Christianity; yet with him there is always a tendency to prefer the poetical to the actual; and it was just for this reason that he had always a greater attraction for the Old Testament than for the New. To both Jacobi and De Wette, Schleiermacher stands immeasurably superior; he is unquestionably the head of his school. In him is represented the whole class of theologians who have sought to rest religion upon heart-perception, and therefore in him we behold the class at its best. We intend in the next chapter to translate into English the thought of Schleiermacher; but before doing so, we wish briefly to inquire into the cause of that wonderful popularity which has placed him at the summit of theological influence. In logical power Schleiermacher is not only not remarkable, but positively deficient. The works which he has left us are a mass of inextricable inconsistencies, which no ingenuity can reconcile and no explanation can torture into harmony. Strauss has not overshot the mark when he says that Schleiermacher betrayed philosophy to theology, and theology to philosophy, for indeed it is his perpetual practice to undo with his left hand what he has accomplished by his right. Nor yet is Schleiermacher remarkable for the originality of his genius; in this respect he is decidedly inferior both to Schelling and Hegel. Nevertheless, how stands the fact? At the present moment, in Germany, the theology of Hegel is rapidly disappearing, and that of Schleiermacher is day by day gathering an increase of strength. That very University of Tübingen, which was a few years ago the hotbed of Hegelianism, is now presided over almost entirely by the school of Schleiermacher. All this demands an explanation, and such an explanation is not at first sight easily to be found. We have said that it lies not in Schleiermacher's superior logic; we have said that it consists not in his superior originality. How, then, are we to account for that wonderful influence which has made him ever increasingly, for the last thirty years, at once the starting-point of religious

Transition to Schleiermacher.

thought and the centre of theological speculation in Germany?

Now it is our opinion that the secret of this influence will be found in Schleiermacher's want of originality, or, to put it more exactly, in the sacrifice of his genius to his sympathy. His aim was not so much to discover anything new, as to find out what was good in the old. His object was to select the best points of each system, and to blend them together into a system of his own. In a review of his opinions, there are two things which candid criticism must ever keep widely separate: we must distinguish between Schleiermacher the religious thinker, and Schleiermacher the scientific theologian. It is the former aspect that constitutes his greatness; it is this which has given him a pre-eminence in Germany. He struck a new key-note amidst the discordant sounds of jarring systems, and sought, instead of founding an additional school, to unite the conflicting schools in the bonds of charity. He felt, and rightly felt, that the spirit of religion itself was deeper than all religions. He perceived by personal experience that Christianity had indeed brought a new and higher life into the world; and he was persuaded, that wherever life exists, it must assimilate everything to itself. It was hence that for the religion of Christ he claimed a wider extent of dominion than had hitherto been yielded to it, and looked forward with eager interest to the time when all intellectual differences would be merged in the unity of love. In all this

Schleiermacher was a pure and sound religious thinker, and deservedly receives our respect and admiration; but when we pass to Schleiermacher as a scientific theologian, we enter into a new and a less genial atmosphere. He was right in his belief that the life of Christ in the world must assimilate to itself all that is good everywhere, but unsuccessful in that method by which he attempted to demonstrate how the assimilation could be achieved; nor, indeed, from his starting-point, could it well be otherwise. If Schleiermacher had founded his Eclecticism merely upon those instincts of the heart which were really the moving-spring of his theology, he would probably have removed himself beyond the reach of criticism. But Schleiermacher did more than that; he made the heart an organ of science. Whatever he believed to lie in the depth of human feeling, he proceeded to formulate into an intellectual proposition; and as from his large-hearted charity he was very apt to feel a certain sympathy with all sincere thought, his theology became very much an affirmation of all opinions. It matters not to him whether or not these different ideas could ever be naturally connected; if they were incapable of union by nature, he tied them together by an artificial string. Intellectual consistency was no object; the only object was to unite all parties, and in this, in an outward sense, he succeeded. Each separate school of theological belief, and of theological unbelief too, was delighted to see itself mirrored in the system of Schleiermacher. There was scarcely a single party which could not claim him for its own. Orthodoxy claimed him, for he certainly started with the most pious intentions. Rationalism claimed him, for he very soon deviated into a path of the wildest speculation. Even the Church of Rome in one aspect could claim him, for he regarded the Church as nothing less than a new incarnation of the risen Jesus. Schleiermacher reminds us very forcibly of an artist, who was so anxious to create a work of universal popularity that he promised to take suggestions from whomsoever they should be offered; he did so, and the picture came out a daub. We do not think that Schleiermacher's scientific theology has been more successful; it is a sad piece of patchwork, in which the most renovated spots of old garments are sewn together, but not in such a way as to prevent the rents from appearing. We doubt if there is a single feature of his system which is distinctively new. Every separate element in it is either an appropriation of contemporary ideas, or but a resurrection of buried forms. His conception of God is certainly not borrowed from his contemporaries, but is a clear revival of Platonism. His doctrine of the impossibility of absolute knowledge for man is an adoption of the Kantian philosophy. His denial of an immanent Trinity is an agreement with the earliest attacks of Rationalism on divine truth. His belief that God becomes conscious of Himself only in the entire race of humanity is in harmony with the worst features of the Hegelian system; nor is this doctrine reconcilable with Schleiermacher's other opinion, that the fulness of the Godhead is embodied in Christ. His estimate of Christ's person itself scarcely rises above the standard of a refined Arianism; nay, in one sense not so high, for it does not appear from Schleiermacher's system that he conceded to Christ any pre-existent life: in this respect he is nearer to the Deist than to the Arian. Thus, gathering its materials from all parts, the theology of Schleiermacher has presented itself to every school of thought as a claimant for its sympathy; and perhaps never in the history of mankind has Eclecticism been favoured with so signal a success. Under the banner of Schleiermacher the partisans of every creed can rank themselves; and his theology, by the fearless sacrifice of all consistency, has extended its arms to embrace all.

With these strictures on the scientific method of Schleiermacher, which yet we do not extend to his religious intention, we proceed, as on the former occasion, to translate his thoughts into English; and in doing so we will follow the plan adopted with reference to Kant—that is to say, we will give in the next chapter a brief outline of Schleiermacher's views under the heads of different doctrines. We shall allow him to speak for himself, not in his own words, but in his own thoughts, reserving only the privilege of translating these thoughts from a German into an English garb.

CHAPTER IV.

THOUGHT-TRANSLATION OF THE SYSTEM OF SCHLEIERMACHER.

I.—NATURE OF GOD.

GOD is that which underlies all things, the unknown unity in which all things are included. Accordingly, Personality is also included in God. Nevertheless, it gives no adequate idea of Him to say that He is a Person; He has an infinite number of manifestations, and Personality is only one amongst the rest. He becomes personal in man, but what He is in Himself is unknowable and inconceivable. All that we are entitled to say of Him is, that He is the Cause of all that exists, the ultimate Force to which everything must be referred.

REMARK.—The student will here observe how close is the resemblance between the God of Schleiermacher and the God of Kant; both have borrowed their conception from the systems of Neo-Platonism.

II.—ATTRIBUTES OF GOD.

God has only one attribute, that of Power or Causality; everything else which we attribute to God is a modification of this. The rays of the sun assume different tints in passing through different objects; so, in like manner, does the one attribute of divine power appear to take different forms, according to the *media* through which it passes. We say, appear to take! because in reality the difference lies not in God, but in our view of Him. We believe that there is an outward object which, when it strikes the eye, produces the sensation of different colours, but we have no right to say that the colours are in the object; they are caused by the object, but they exist in the eye. Even so the attributes of God are certain mental sensations or feelings produced by the unknown Cause of all things. When we see the Cause acting on material things, we call it physical force; but it does not follow that physical force is in the Cause itself. When we feel it acting upon our own spirits, we call it divine wisdom; it produces in us the idea of intelligence, and we transfer that idea to the Cause: this, however, we have no right to do. When it acts upon our moral nature, we call it divine holiness; it wakens within us the idea of conscience, and we transfer this idea also to the source which gave it: it is, however, only an effect, and gives no indication whatever of the character of its author. Or yet again, when we see it acting in the retributions of

Attributes of God. 43

life, that is to say, in the constant connection of suffering with sin, we call it divine justice; the truth being, that the unknown Cause, by the very connection of sin with suffering, has awakened in us the idea of justice. When we think of the Cause itself, and consider how through all changes it abides immutable, we attribute to it the quality of eternal existence, this thought being the product of its continual action on our minds. It is thus that the attributes of God are nothing more than views of Him from different human standpoints, the various appearances which the one changeless Cause presents to our finite intelligence according as we look at it from different sides of the spiritual landscape. God in Himself is an unchangeable unity, incapable of variation, and without any possibility of distinctions in His nature. He is the same yesterday, and to-day, and for ever; and if we attribute to Him a yesterday, a to-day, or a for ever, it can only be received as a representation in the language of men.

REMARK.—Unsatisfactory to the religious mind as is Schleiermacher's conception of a God without attributes, we yet believe he was led to it by a high religious motive,—the desire to exalt Christ. We think he wished to show how impossible to such a being as man would have been any knowledge of God, or even any reasonable imagination of Him, had He not been manifested in the personal life of the Redeemer. This is only one of the many instances in which we must separate Schleiermacher the religious thinker, from Schleiermacher the scientific theologian.

III.—CREATION OF MAN.

Man had a beginning, but whether or not the world had must ever remain doubtful. What we mean by the creation of the world is the fact that the world lives, and moves, and has its being in God. This does not of necessity imply that it ever began to be; it only amounts to this, that at no moment of its being could it exist without God, that God is its life and its eternal support. There is thus no real distinction between preservation and creation; God's preservation of the universe may be said to be a new creation of it out of nothing every moment, for it can only be preserved by receiving each instant a fresh influx of the divine life. But while there is no necessity to suppose a beginning of the world, there is an absolute necessity to suppose a beginning of Man; for we see that the life of Man belongs to a higher order than that of the world, and therefore could never be generated by it. There must, therefore, at one time have been a miracle, an interruption of the ordinary course of things, by which a new and higher life was imparted to the world, and it was rendered capable of advancing farther into the realization of the divine ideal: this new life was the creation of Man.

IV.—THE FALL.

Man was created with two natures; one was of the earth, and the other from heaven. The earthly nature tended to bind him to the things of sense; the heavenly one filled him with the thoughts of God. Both of these natures were good when considered separately. Evil arises not from either of them in itself, but from the meeting and conflict of the two. The earth-nature is perfectly good in an animal, because it is the law of its being. But in Man the earth-nature comes into collision with a higher law, and therefore it ought to yield to it. It so happens, however, that at the beginning of life the senses have got the start of the spirit. In childhood we are entirely occupied with sensuous impressions, and on this account the earth-nature has the advantage of a more lengthened development within us than the heavenly one. No sooner do these natures come into union than they come into conflict; the flesh lusteth against the spirit, and the spirit against the flesh; and because the flesh has got the start of the spirit, it gains a temporary victory. Hence the Fall of man speedily followed his creation; the heavenly nature was vanquished, and he became the slave of sense. In this state of things something must be done to supply the place of a heavenly motive. Man cannot will the good for its own sake; he must, therefore, be deterred from the evil by the fear of punishment. In the Old Testament suffering is always connected with sin, and every deed meets with its just retribution. The reason is plain. In the Old Testament, Man is so corrupt that he is incapable of seeing the intrinsic beauty of virtue; he cannot seek the right, he can only be frightened from the wrong. The Old Testament, therefore, is a dispensation of outward rewards and punishments; but the very fact that man needs such a dispensation is a proof of universal corruption. The corruption could not be otherwise than universal. The sin by which Man fell was not the sin of an individual, but of the whole race. For that which we call humanity is not merely the general name for a series of individuals; it is a real collective substance, an essence, of which the individuals are only accidents. Hence one man could not fall without dragging down all humanity along with him; for every man is only one part or fragment of a great connected life, which unites in itself all other lives. For the same reason, if one man should ever conquer temptation, and exhibit a perfect purity, he could not do so alone; the whole united mass would be lifted up along with him, and redemption would be secured. But where shall we find a perfect man amidst this corruption generated by the Fall? Is there any possibility of this life retrieving its lost glory by its own inward strength? No; it is impossible. What then? There must be a second miracle; God must again interfere. As a miracle was necessary to Man's creation, it must be repeated to secure his redemption. The first miracle brought a new life to nature; the second must convey a new life to Man.

REMARK.—Schleiermacher is here more orthodox than Kant, inasmuch as he does not admit Man's ability to redeem himself, but recognises the necessity for a supernatural interference. Be it observed, however, that with Schleiermacher there is no absolute miracle. The miracles of Man's creation and Man's redemption were, according to him, bound up in the original constitution of things, and were intended to occur at a specified time; he thus regards miracles as parts of the law of nature. Man is created in order that he may fall, and he falls in order that he may be redeemed. On this point Schleiermacher is an extreme Calvinist.

V.—PERSON OF CHRIST.

The effect of the second miracle is the manifestation of Christ. Christ is at once above humanity and in union with humanity. On the one hand, He never could have come into the world by a natural process;— the proof of this is, that His life impresses us with an exalted feeling, which altogether transcends our own capacity. But on the other hand, Christ is essentially human. He is the Archetype of humanity, its pattern, its ideal. When God said, 'Let us make Man,' His thought was pointing, not to Man at his beginning, but to Man at his climax; not to the first, but to the second Adam; not to humanity unfallen, but to humanity redeemed. Christ, therefore, was the goal of creation; and being its goal, He was also its beginning, for that which is last in realization is first in thought. Just as, in a work of fiction, all the incidents are subservient to the conclusion, and the working out of that conclusion is the first thing present to the mind of the author, even so in the drama of this universe, the completed idea is the earliest object of divine thought, and all other things are only valuable because they lead up to that. The opening buds of spring derive their value from being the harbingers of the summer's glory; even so, in the divine thought, this world obtained a borrowed lustre from the forecast shadow of the perfect fruit which was to spring from the tree of life. Christ, therefore, while in one sense He is above humanity, is yet in another the only true Man, because He is the Archetype of human nature, and the original pattern after whose image and likeness the human race was fashioned.

VI.—Redemption.

Christ, then, has become Man. He has come in an individual form; but, as already said, He could not become one man without becoming all humanity. Humanity is, as we have seen, not a mere series of individuals, but a connected mass. It is like the ocean, which, while it holds within itself a myriad of individual drops, is yet a continuous whole. Christ, therefore, by taking a human form, united Himself to the whole mass of human nature, and lifted it up to His own level. He elevated our humanity not so much by doing anything for it, as by simply living in it. His life came into contact with our nature like a fire, and our nature caught the spark, and propagated it. We became inoculated, so to speak, with a new substance,—a substance which had the tendency to drive out the old germs of disease, and to prevent them from ever again finding a place within us. This was the true work of the Son of man. He became what we are, that He might make us what He is. Nevertheless, Christ could not do this without suffering; He could not take up our human nature without taking up its sorrows too. If a perfect head were attached to a diseased body, the head would inevitably be affected by the body; it would bear the consequences of its disease. Now that is just the Pauline figure. Christ is the head, and we are the members. The head is perfectly free from imperfection, but the members are pervaded with disease. Accordingly, when the head comes into union with the members, it must suffer along with them; we are the body of Christ, and He bears the sins and infirmities of our body. Yet this suffering is in Christ vicarious. We have seen that in the Old Testament suffering was attached to sin as a deterrent motive. In the New Testament this connection is dissolved. Christ comes into the world perfectly sinless—indeed it is His sinlessness which constitutes His divinity. Accordingly, suffering to Him has no longer the same meaning. It comes to Him not as a punishment, but as something which was once intended as a punishment to others, and which remains in the world merely as the relic of a past age. It was Christ's glory to discover that to every good man suffering is henceforth vicarious—that it is no longer the mark of God's anger, but merely something which must be borne as a memorial of our fallen condition. In a word, it was the prerogative of Christ, and it is the prerogative of the Christian, to experience that the sufferings which still cling to his nature were not meant for him, but for others; this is the true significance of vicarious satisfaction.

VII.—THE CHURCH, AND THE TRINITY COMPLETED.

We have now seen God in two aspects. We have seen Him as the unknown unity which underlies all things, and we have seen Him coming into conscious personality in the human life of Christ. But a third aspect remains to complete the Trinity, and that is the life of the risen Christ in the Church.

When Christ ascended from the grave, He passed into a new incarnation. He was no longer embodied in a merely individual form, but became a divine essence in the hearts of all His people. This new incarnation of Christ in the entire mass of believers is what is called the Church, and forms the transition to the dispensation of the Spirit. The Holy Spirit is neither more nor less than the life of Christ repeated in the inward experience of His followers. Here, as in the individual form, Christ again passes through a series of gradations, advances through childhood and youth up to maturity, and reaches His human development through struggle and suffering. The life of the Church, which is a repetition of the life of Christ, must arrive at its manhood through a slow and tedious progress, and attain the fulness of its life by surmounting the limitations incidental to each stage of its being. What, then, is the evidence that we are members of this Church? It is the possession of the spirit of religion; and religion is the feeling of absolute dependence on God. The only infinite thing about Man is his helplessness, and therefore he only becomes strong when he realizes his perfect weakness. Sin manifests itself in the effort after self-activity. Man tries to support himself without the aid of God. He only returns to himself when he gives up the false activity in exchange for the true dependence; for by losing his own individual life he becomes partaker of that great generic life which the risen Christ has diffused throughout the world, and in entering into fellowship with the united Church he has become recipient of the life of the Redeemer.

SUMMARY OF RESULTS.

Such is the result of an attempt to establish scientific theology upon a basis of pure feeling. It must be evident to all that the aim has not succeeded. We concede to Schleiermacher the purest religious intention. We believe that his errors were rather intellectual than spiritual. We grant that to a great extent his own warmth of heart and widespread charity contributed to revivify the religious life of Germany. We can, even in many of his dogmatic statements, discern much that is true and much that is valuable; and those parts of his system which want these qualities perhaps owe their imperfection chiefly to the inadequacy of the understanding to express the instincts of the heart. It cannot be denied, indeed, that if we take one by one the different parts of his theology, we shall find many things which we must pronounce good; Schleiermacher could not possibly have given utterance to so many isolated sentiments without flashing out here and there a great verity. In this sense, much that he has written does indeed make an appeal to human feeling. But the difficulty of following Schleiermacher lies in this, that the sentiments to which he gives utterance *are* isolated; they are in no way connected with one another, but are merely tied together like a string of pearls. Nay, they are not only unconnected, in many instances they are positively at variance. Schleiermacher starts from the reverence of Christian feeling, and from such a starting-point one would have expected that he would have found a God of love. Instead of that, his first principle is an unknown unity,—a force which is manifested everywhere, but which is itself discoverable

Summary of Results. 53

nowhere. In accordance with his Christian feeling, he professes unbounded devotion to the person of the Redeemer; indeed, it is not without reason that Strauss has said of him, 'He had no God but Christ.' And yet, when we come to inquire into his idea of Christ, we are at a loss to discover wherein to Schleiermacher consists His glory. It nowhere appears that he regards Him as a pre-existent Being. He concedes, no doubt, that His origin was in some sense miraculous, but he does not seem to have admitted His eternity in the past. Even the earthly Christ is with him not so much a historical as an ideal existence; like Kant, he is prone to disparage the value of external facts. He admits, for instance, the historical truth of Christ's resurrection, but he denies that the Christian religion is in any sense affected either by its truth or falsity. He rejects the opening narratives of Matthew and Luke, reduces the temptation to one of our Lord's parables exhibiting the course of the divine life, prunes down the gospel miracles into manifestations of unknown laws, and in general mutilates the main features of the whole picture. Nor does it very clearly appear whether his Christ has any greater claim to futurity than to pre-existence. Is the Christ of Schleiermacher at this moment a living Being? That question does not seem to be answered by his system. He tells us, no doubt, that the ascended Christ lives again in the life of the Church, but in one sense this might be said of every saint and martyr whose work has been the means of advancing the cause of truth.

There is a sense in which it may be said of all the departed, that, being dead, they yet speak to us, for after death our influence remains either for good or evil. Is this all that Schleiermacher means by the assertion that Christ lives again in His Church? Probably not; it is more than likely that his words have a deeper significance. But even admitting that the life of Christ in the Church is with Schleiermacher a real thing, what does such a statement amount to? Merely that through the body of Christian believers there is diffused a mysterious divine essence, uncomprehended and incomprehensible. Will such a conception supply to the Christian consciousness the place of a personal risen Redeemer? Is the object which the Christian seeks nothing more than an abstract conviction that in some unknown manner he is partaker of that divine spark which dwelt in Jesus of Nazareth? Can any man read the earliest Christian records, and fail to be impressed with the belief that when they spoke of a risen Redeemer they meant a risen person?

And if we are persuaded that such was the original feeling of the early Church, we cannot but discover a radical inconsistency in a system which, professing to start from obedience to this feeling, ends by refining it away into an empty abstraction. It is true, Schleiermacher does not deny a personal living Redeemer, but neither does he admit Him; on such a Christ he is silent—He has no part in his system. Indeed, on the whole subject of a personal immortality, Schleiermacher is vague and unsatisfactory; he seems to think

Summary of Results.

that the doctrine of a future state must be believed on the authority of Christ alone. For himself, the subject has no theological interest. Although his standpoint professes to be that of individual feeling, he cares little or nothing for the interests of the individual; the race, humanity at large, the collective life of the Church,—these and such as these are the expressions which most frequently fall from him. Redemption itself is viewed rather as something to come than as something completed. It is a small thing to him that individual men should pass away, if humanity itself should be enriched by the fruits of their existence; a small thing that suffering should remain to men as individuals, if it be taken away from humanity as a whole. Therefore, for the individual believer, the Christ of Schleiermacher has little or no significance; He exists only for that world of which the believer is a unit, an atom, a drop in its ocean, a grain-sand on its shore.

There is one other point in which the student must have observed a radical inconsistency in the system of Schleiermacher. His God is not essentially a person; personality is indeed one of His attributes or manifestations, yet it does not touch the nature of His deepest being. Nevertheless, the actions of this impersonal God are such as only a person could perform. He has an archetype of creation which He longs to realize in actual life, and in order to realize it He twice interferes with that course of nature which He has established. He has a definite plan for the development of human nature; and when that nature has fallen, He supports it in its period of degeneracy by attaching to the commission of sin the experience of retributive pain. These are not the acts which we should have expected from an impersonal and an unknown God. We should have looked for them and have expected to find them in an infinitely wise and loving Father. The God of Schleiermacher is neither, yet Schleiermacher assigns Him the prerogatives of both. How are we to account for such inconsistency as this? How otherwise than by the old experience, that a man's heart is often sounder than his head and better than his creed? For let us never forget that it is just the inconsistencies of Schleiermacher which have made him popular. If he had followed out his premises to their logical conclusions, he would have been an object for the prayers of the pious, and his name would have been transmitted to posterity as a mark for religious execration. The foundation on which he built his temple ought to have yielded no other superstructure than the last results of the system of Strauss. But Schleiermacher had a heart, and his heart struggled against his logic. His earliest years had been passed amid the Moravian brotherhood; he was the child of pious parents, and had early received a bias favourable to a religious life. Through all his after years he was never able to shake off these first impressions; they blended even with his most speculative moments, and in the long-run achieved the victory. Schleiermacher was personally a religious man, and the religion of his theology survived its philosophy. The speculative part of his system has well-nigh passed away; few at any time ever adopted it. But these portions of his creed which appeal to the heart of man, these sentiments which are founded upon the intuitions of an earnest and fervent spirit,—these are the reminiscences which have endeared the memory of Schleiermacher to the heart of Germany; and by these he, being dead, yet speaketh.

CHAPTER V.

DIVERSITIES IN THE SCHOOL OF SCHLEIERMACHER.

TO say you are a follower of Schleiermacher is very nearly as vague a statement as to say you are a Protestant. The question always recurs, What particular part of his system do you follow? The theology of Schleiermacher includes every possible opinion; it is a blanket under which infidelity and pietism may sleep side by side. The Germans themselves have ranked his adherents under two great classes,—the believing and the unbelieving theologians; but between these extremes there are many other votaries of this school, who occupy a border-land of mingled light and darkness. The one common element which unites them is the starting-point of individual feeling, and it is not surprising that from such a starting-point the conclusions arrived at should be not only various, but contrary. There are, perhaps, no two men who feel precisely alike. Most men, indeed, take their individual feelings for universal intuitions; but the very contrariety of these dispels the illusion. There is no part of our nature which stands more in need of correction than what we call feeling. Even in its most external form, that of

Diversities in Schleiermacher's School. 59

taste, or the sense of the beautiful, the perceptions of feeling cannot be made authoritative beyond the individual mind; what one man pronounces lovely, another calls insipid. If we ascend into the moral sphere, we meet with a similar experience; all men are agreed that there is a difference between right and wrong, but there is a very great disagreement as to what constitutes the difference. There are many savage tribes who eulogise certain actions which civilised nations would pronounce execrable; and if we are persuaded that the civilised nations have formed the true estimate of the matter, they have certainly not done so from having stronger feelings than the savages, but rather because they have ceased to be ruled by individual feelings, and have adopted universal judgments. And need we add, that in religion it is the same as in morality? There is not a single worshipper on earth whose heart does not tell him that his is the only true religion, or at least more true than any other; and if very often we see men arriving at broader and more catholic views, it is just because they have subordinated the individual impressions of the heart to the universal maxims of intuitive reason. From all this it is manifest that any theology which professes to have its foundation in feeling must inevitably break up into a multitude of divergent systems, and disappear amidst the diversities which its own standpoint has created. It has been so in a pre-eminent degree with the theology of Schleiermacher. As the flood of sunshine, which pours itself over earth and sea and sky, becomes in the very process broken up into scattered rays, each of which takes a different hue, according to the object which it illumines; even so this theology, professing to pour forth a sunshine of universal feeling, breaks itself against the barriers of logical difficulty, and is parted asunder into a multitude of conflicting fragments. Its design is on a level with divinity, but its accomplishment is a product of the dust.

We have said that few have ever embraced the entire theology of Schleiermacher. Perhaps the man who has followed him most closely is Schweizer, who may be taken as representing the theology on its speculative or unbelieving side. At the opposite pole from him stands Tholuck, who is the representative of all that is highest in this system, and who, indeed, has nothing in common with it beyond the starting-point of pious feeling. Between these extreme lines there are many intermediate ones, partaking more or less of the nature of both. Under these circumstances, we have thought it right to occupy the remaining portion of this chapter in giving the student a doctrinal table of what seem to us to be the principal diversities in the school of Schleiermacher. We will endeavour to exhibit these divergences as they occur under the heads of different doctrines, and the student will have an opportunity of marking how wide is that ground which is covered by this school.

I.—NATURE OF GOD.

On this point few agree with Schleiermacher; those, perhaps, who come nearest to him are De Wette, Ewald, and Schweizer. The large majority of the school, as Neander, Twesten, Lücke, Nitzsch, and Ullmann, are Theists.

II.—THE TRINITY.

It will be remembered that the Trinity of Schleiermacher is not a difference in the nature of God Himself, but only a threefold manner in which He manifests Himself in the course of history; his Trinity consists of God in the world, God in Christ, and God in the Church. With this view of a Trinity in history agree De Wette, Twesten, Lücke, and Hase; others, like Nitzsch, make the trinity immanent in the nature of God. There is a class of theologians, represented by Dorner, Martensen, Liebner, Rothe, and Lange, who are generally referred to the school of Schleiermacher, and who have adopted the Hegelian Trinity, to be afterwards described. We shall hereafter show, however, that they more strictly belong to a third party, intermediate between the two Hegelian schools. Their only connection with Schleiermacher lies in the fact that they make Christian feeling their standpoint. Hence to them the essence of God is love, and out of this they make a trinity. Dorner says that love requires two, and love itself, being the union of these two, is the third or completing element. Martensen tries to show that love requires three, a third object being needed to prevent the attraction of the other two from being a necessity. The view of Weisse is peculiar. He adopts a trinity of persons, yet he does not make Christ the second Person. According to him, the second Person of the Trinity loses His personality at the creation, and becomes identified with the world; His personality, however, will be restored when the world has been redeemed.

REMARK.—In placing Dorner, Martensen, and Lange in this category, we would not be misunderstood. The aim of these theologians was deeper than the reconciliation of intellectual schools of thought. What we have called their Hegelianism was rather a framework than a basis. Knowing that the Christian life must breathe a certain atmosphere of culture, they have naturally sought to appropriate and modify to a healthy temperature the existing atmosphere of their country. Yet at the basis of their system there is found something which belongs to them more distinctively than either to Hegel or Schleiermacher,—a reference to Scripture as an ultimate authority. Dorner exhibits Scripture in its historical development; Martensen views it in its relation to reason and morality; while Lange, whose commentaries are amongst the most valuable contributions to biblical literature, seeks to illustrate and unfold the harmony of its various parts and the rich fulness of its spiritual teaching.

III.—ATTRIBUTES OF GOD.

We saw that Schleiermacher made all the divine attributes modifications of power; Rothe makes them modifications of omniscience. According to him, omniscience is causative; that is to say, God's foreknowledge that a thing will be causes it to be. As this might tend to make God the author of sin, Rothe denies that His omniscience can extend to concrete events, but limits it to the abstract plan of the universe. It is to be remarked that the school of Schleiermacher in general regards sin as something outside the power of the divine attributes—in other words, as incomprehensible even to God, and therefore incapable of being either foreseen or prevented by Him. In this respect the school has departed from the Calvinism of its master, who fearlessly included sin in the plan of the universe.

IV.—IMMORTALITY.

This doctrine, as we have seen, was received by Schleiermacher purely on the authority of Christ; he found no place for it in the nature of things. Olshausen has gone still further. He has denied the possibility of a soul existing apart from a body, and therefore has maintained that, previous to the resurrection, the spirit of man can only live in union with the particles of the body, either in the grave or scattered throughout the universe. Weisse and Rothe refuse to admit a universal immortality, but consider eternal life as the exclusive possession of the redeemed. There is, of course, a sense in which every Christian holds the same, but with these theologians eternal life is that which in the future will supply the place of this natural existence, and without which there could be no future life at all. With the exception, however, of these extravagances, there is, on the whole, a preponderance of orthodox opinion regarding this doctrine.

V.—Origin of Evil.

We saw that Schleiermacher makes sin descend generically from the first man; and in this he is followed by all who hold that humanity is a connected whole,—a class which certainly comprehends the large majority of German theologians. The most remarkable divergence from this view is the theory of Julius Müller, who denies the generic unity of humanity, and regards the race as nothing more than a series of individuals. He holds that each of these individuals must at one time have had the power of an unbiased choice between good and evil, for without such a choice he considers that man could not be held responsible for his sins. But where shall we find any period of life in which we are unbiased between good and evil? Müller admits that we cannot do so. Go back so far as he will, he discovers in man a nature already formed. Shall he seek it, then, at the dawn of childhood? But of this memory gives him no knowledge, and, moreover, he cannot believe that God would place the power of choice in the weak will of a child. Accordingly, Müller goes back further still,—beyond the earth, beyond time, beyond our present consciousness,—to an unknown and departed life, which the soul enjoyed previous to its entrance into this mortal body. Here we had full power of choice between the alternatives of right and wrong; and, by making our choice on the side of wrong, we have been punished by falling into the bondage of our present existence. The student will here remark something like a return to the philosophy of Kant.

VI.—PERSON OF CHRIST.

Not only Schleiermacher, but in general German theologians of every school have denied the existence of two separate natures in Christ. Dorner makes this dogma the leading reason why Christ in thought has been made distant to the soul. The formula of German theologians on this subject might be thus paraphrased in English: Christ has one nature, which is either human or divine, according to the side from which we contemplate it; human, because kindred to our humanity; divine, because exhibiting our humanity in perfection. This theory is clearly founded on the assumption that perfect humanity would be equal to God. But even if this point were conceded, we would by no means discover in German theology any unanimous verdict regarding the place in creation of this

66 Diversities in Schleiermacher's School.

divinely human Person. On this point the school of Schleiermacher is especially discordant. Schleiermacher himself placed the divinity of Christ in His sinlessness; and in this he was followed by Schweizer, Hase, and Ullmann. Weisse and Ewald assign Him merely a relative divinity. He is with them the sum of God's revelation in relation to the present world. A far higher place is accorded to Him by Dorner, Rothe, Martensen, Liebner, and Lange, all of whom regard Christ as the head of a universal organism; but their view cannot be made clear to the student until he has become familiar with that system of Hegel which we have elsewhere to describe. There is one point, however, which must at present be taken into consideration, because it constitutes one of the most radical differences which exist between Schleiermacher and his school. It will be remembered that Schleiermacher made the incarnation of Christ the result of human sin. In this he is followed by few. The general tendency of German theology is to regard the incarnation as something which would have happened even if Man had never fallen. Indeed, the only writers of any eminence whom we know to have taken a contrary view are Müller and Thomasius. Müller holds humanity to be merely a series of individuals, and therefore, in his view, Christ can have no necessary connection with it. Thomasius believes, indeed, that humanity is an organic whole, but considers its natural head to have been not Christ, but Adam. German theology has in general sketched out a grander destiny for Man. It has refused to believe that even in the morning of his creation he had reached his goal. It has refused to accept the first Adam as God's ideal for humanity, but has contemplated the Son of man as all along the design and pattern after which it was made. It regards the first creation as imperfect from the beginning; it was only Man in the image of God. To complete the work of the six days, another work remained,—the appearance of God in the image of Man. Therefore to German theology the incarnation is a necessary thing—necessary not alone as the result of sin, but as the result of life, not to accomplish Man's redemption, but to complete his creation. The coming of the Son of God is alone the perfect fulfilment of the mandate, 'Let us make man.'

How, then, does God become Man? Schleiermacher has not answered this question; he is content to feel it, without reasoning about it. But his followers have tried to answer it for him, and in doing so they have again divided the camp of their general. Dorner, with whom Martensen agrees, considers that the eternal Logos, or pre-existent nature of Jesus, remained unchanged at His incarnation, but merely poured forth into His human soul so much light as would render it perfect at each stage of its being. Christ, as a child, was possessed of perfection—that is to say, He was a perfect child; but He could not at the same moment be a perfect man. Every sphere into which His human life passed added perfection to perfection. He did not fill all at once, but He filled up each to the full.

This view of Dorner, however, has found few supporters in Germany. Thomasius, Gess, Lange, and the large majority of evangelical theologians have refused to admit that the pre-existent nature of Jesus could remain unchanged at His incarnation. They have refused to do so on the ground that such a theory would deprive the incarnation of its value. It is clear to them that the coming to earth of the Son of man is represented in the Bible as a sacrifice, and that if it were a sacrifice, it must have involved the giving up of something which was a part of His nature. Accordingly, these theologians have adopted a view of Christ's incarnation which in this country is comparatively unknown. They hold that the pre-existent Christ emptied Himself not of any outward majesty, but of His own life. He broke that bond of connection which had bound Him to the Father. He snapped the chain of consciousness which had made Him one with God. He forgot the heavenly life which He had enjoyed in the bosom of the Father, forgot it utterly and entirely, and began a new life in which He had no remembrance of it. By a voluntary surrender of His divine will He fell asleep, and woke again in a new form and with a new life, not as the heir of eternity, but with the heart and the intelligence of a little child. This is what is meant when it is said, 'He humbled Himself; He made Himself of no reputation.' His human birth was a sleep and a forgetting; His entrance into time was the death of His life in eternity. Henceforth He must begin anew, must grow like other children, must learn like other children, must pass like others through the stages of human development, until at last His humanity reaches that very point which His divine life had abandoned, and the Son of man attains through struggle that unity with God which He had originally by nature. Such is the common theory of the evangelical party in the school of Schleiermacher. Ebrard, indeed, has attempted to modify it by the paradox of a double consciousness in Jesus, by which the heavenly memory could subsist along with the earthly life, but his views on this point have nowhere found acceptance. It remains that we notice one other doctrinal variety in the school of Schleiermacher, after which we shall have enumerated at once the main features of his system and the principal points in which the disciples diverge from the master.

VII.—REDEMPTION.

The student will remember that Schleiermacher made redemption not something done *for* Man, but a work done *in* him. Christ assumed the nature not of a single individual, but of all mankind; and by uniting Himself to humanity, He lifted it up to His own level. This view is not peculiar to Schleiermacher, but is common to the whole range of German theology. The doctrine of a vicarious substitution is almost unknown in Germany. We say almost, because there is one branch of the school of Schleiermacher which in this respect has separated itself from the parent tree, and approached more nearly to the English standpoint; the representatives of this small party are Delitzsch and Ebrard. These theologians have adopted the common English view, that the death of Christ was an expiatory sacrifice for the sins of the world. In one respect, indeed, they differ from that standpoint. It is the doctrine of English theology that the righteousness of Christ is imputed to the believer previous to his own sanctification. Delitzsch and Ebrard do not admit this, but hold that by the death of Christ Man has received nothing but pardon for the past; he is not counted righteous, but merely forgiven. His righteousness only comes when he is made partaker of Christ's actual nature. This takes place when the believer receives at communion His mystical body and blood; for there is then imparted to him a new substance, a divine element different from either soul or body, a third part of his nature, which he possessed before the Fall, and by which he enjoyed direct communion with Heaven, which was rent from him by the loss of Eden, and is restored to him by communion with the Son of man. Delitzsch and Ebrard, therefore, will not concede that God will declare Man righteous unless he actually be righteous; the merits of Christ must be in him before they can be imputed to him. Tholuck, who belongs to this party, has attempted to show that there is no difference, in God's sight, between the imputation of righteousness and the possession of righteousness; for with God, to think is to create, to declare a thing to be is to cause it to be. This mode of putting the matter is a curious illustration of the fact that the idealism of Hegel has penetrated, consciously or unconsciously, into the most evangelical forms of German theology, and suffused the opinions of those who are most vehement against it. Delitzsch and Ebrard, with their third part added to human nature, and Tholuck, with his doctrine that declaration is equal to creation, are fine examples of the truth that the theology of Schleiermacher has been unable to subsist upon the food of pious emotion.

CHAPTER VI.

FICHTE.

WE shall now recall the mind of the student to that point from which we started at the opening of the third chapter. We there saw that Kant had left everything in a state of negation; Rationalism had been destroyed, and nothing else had as yet been set up in its room. We saw that in such times of negation there must always predominate one or other of two tendencies,—either the clinging to the testimony of faith, or the abandonment to the recklessness of despair. We saw that in Germany the philosophy of Kant had given rise to both of these tendencies, and we proposed in turn to exhibit the nature and results of each. We found that the first, that of implicit faith, had assumed two forms, according as it placed the ground of faith in the authority of an infallible Church, or in the testimony of religious feeling. Dismissing the former as outside the range of German theology, we proceeded to take up the latter, as represented by the system of Schleiermacher; and after a brief review of that system, we have found ourselves in a condition to judge of its results. From a scientific

Fichte. 73

point of view, the verdict must be unfavourable; and we are bound to confess, that the standpoint of religious feeling has failed to fill up the blank created by the destructiveness of the Kantian Philosophy. We are now driven, therefore, to the second of these parallel lines which proceeded from the anarchy raised by the destruction of Rationalism. This second tendency is the scepticism of despair, and it finds its representative in Fichte. Fichte was not a theologian; his whole importance for us lies in the fact that he forms a transition point between destruction and reconstruction: he occupies that border-land of negation which always intervenes between the passing away of old things and the becoming of all things new. With Fichte we begin to see the dawn of hope; but it is only because he has reached so low a stage that we cannot imagine a worse, and because we have an instinctive feeling that when things have reached the worst they begin to mend. Not that the system of Fichte breathes the spirit of melancholy; it is despair, indeed, but despair in its recklessness; it is perplexity, but perplexity drowning itself with laughter. The philosophy of Fichte exhibits the appearance of a false emancipation; it is the freedom of the libertine, who exults in his own lawlessness. For the rest, it is, perhaps, the nearest approach to absolute scepticism which the world has ever seen. Let us first consider its relation to that philosophy which preceded it. Kant had laboured to demonstrate that what we call the axioms of reason are the contradictions of reason, that no testimony derived from outward experience is of any value, and that the very existence of effects and causes is an idea thrust upon nature by the human mind. Fichte accepted his conclusions; but he could not stop there. He saw clearly, that if there be nothing in the universe corresponding to effects and causes, there is no reason left for a universe at all. That which we call nature, viewed on its mechanical side, is nothing more than a system, or correlation, of causes and effects; and if this correlation be proved to be no part of nature, what remains to nature other than the name? Such was the reasoning of Fichte; and considering the premises from which he started, we cannot say that he reasoned illogically. Kant had reduced nature to a minimum. He had torn from it all those qualities which we are accustomed to attribute to external objects. He had not only abstracted from it what we call its secondary qualities,—heat, cold, hardness, softness, colour, sound, and the like—to go thus far was perfectly philosophical,—but Kant had gone further; he had maintained that the very forms of things were mental conceptions, in which the spirit clothed the objects of sensation. The strange thing was, that, having gone so far, Kant was content to stop before he reached his destination. He still professed to believe in an outward world, even after he had rent that world into fragments. He had deprived it of every possible quality which could make it real; yet he professed to believe that he had left something undestroyed, that there still remained without us an unknown and unknowable substance, to which we might give the name of matter. Fichte said, Why cling to the existence of that which is unknowable? why adhere to the name when you havé taken away the thing? You say that all our experiences of the outer world are merely forms of thought which the mind impresses upon that world; why, then, speak of a world at all? why say that there is anything apart from the mind? why not reduce everything within the dominion of the spirit?

Such was the aim of Fichte. He proposed to carry out to the uttermost those principles which Kant had enunciated; and he felt, and rightly felt, that if the principles of Kant were true, they must reach further than he carried them. Fichte determined to begin where Kant had ended, and therefore he made his starting-point the non-existence of an outward world. The formula in which he expresses this is contained in the words, 'the Ego is one and all.' Now let us translate this formula into English. It clearly means two things: first, that there is nothing in the universe but mind, what he calls the Ego; and secondly, that there is only one mind in the universe. Perhaps the latter point is the more original. The idea that there is no such thing as matter was far from a new thought, and had existed in England before it found expression in Germany. But there is something peculiarly startling in the doctrine of Fichte that there is only one mind in the universe. It is commonly computed that there are upwards of nine hundred millions of human beings on the globe; but Fichte tells us that this is a mistake, there is in truth only one. The unsophisticated listener who has not yet become familiar with this transcendentalism is inclined to ask, Who is this favoured being? is it you or I, or some third party? But, indeed, such a question is itself a proof that the listener is only on the threshold of the subject; if he studies it more deeply, he will find that he has mistaken Fichte's standpoint. In the system of Fichte there is no difference recognised between you and me. There is only one being in the universe; and if that being were perfect, he would have no sense of anything out of himself. It is only because he is imperfect that he imagines himself to be split up into different individuals. He experiences within himself something which resists his progress and prevents him from realizing his full being, and accordingly he thinks of this inward resistance as if it were something over against him and external to him. This is the reason why the Ego or universal mind conceives itself to be divided into a number of isolated individuals, each seeking to subsist independently of the other, and even by the destruction of the other. Now this strange theory of Fichte's has been dignified with the name of spiritual Pantheism. It is most unfair to call it so. There is a sense in which spiritual Pantheism exists even in the Bible,—the sense in which Paul says that in Him we live, and move, and have our being. But so far from holding this, the system of Fichte does not admit that we live, and move, and have our being at all; it does not admit the existence in the universe of such beings as we; it acknowledges only the life of one mind. Now this is not Pantheism, either spiritual or material. Pantheism has many forms, but to all its forms there is one common idea—that all things live in God. But in this system of Fichte's there is no all, there is only one. Pantheism, in its highest form, is quite consistent with the belief in a personal God; but the one solitary mind of Fichte is not a God in any sense. It cannot be called a supreme power, for there is nothing beneath it; it cannot be termed a providence, for it has nothing to provide for; it cannot be named the creator, because in this world of Fichte's there is no creation—nay, there is no existence but the one solitary mind. Such a doctrine can manifestly receive only one name, and that name is not Pantheism, but Atheism. Fichte, on the side of spiritualism, has arrived at the same miserable goal which was afterwards reached by Comte on the side of materialism,— a world whose essence is unknown, but above which there can be nothing.[1]

But Fichte now goes on to relate the history of this Ego, this solitary mind of the universe. He tells us that it passes through five stages. It begins with the life of instinct, when it exists without knowing its existence. Its character at this stage is that of boundless spontaneity, of perfect liberty, of freedom from all restraint. By and by there comes a change. The instinctive life meets with a check, a barrier, a limit

[1] See supplementary note, page 190.

to its progress; the age of liberty is past, and the age of authority is come. But the life which was once free revolts from this authority, and therefore there opens upon it a third and stormier period,—the time of anarchy, revolution, opposition to all existing things. When the anarchy has run its course, when licence is weary of its own lawlessness, then the age of reason comes. Last of all, reason itself gives place to intuition, and truth is sought no longer by the steps of a ladder, but by its own inherent light: this is the perfect life of the soul. Such are the five stages of Fichte. Every man knows that these progressive phases of being are found in individual experience, and it is from individual experience that Fichte has borrowed them. But Fichte says that whatever exists in the individual must be transferred to the universal mind. He tells us that the existence of the individual is a delusion, a dream, an imagination, and that we ought to forget this delusion in the sense of our unity with the universal mind. I and my Father are one; that, says Fichte, is what every man should be able to declare. The glory of Christ was that He was the first to discover the non-existence of His own individual nature, the first to proclaim to the world the eternal truth that there is only one Spirit in the universe, and that we have no life apart from that Spirit. This was the truth which the Son of man discovered, and every one who discovers it after Him shall be likewise a Son of man; for Christ is in this respect not superior to humanity, but rather the ideal and exemplar of what all humanity should be and shall be. We become the sons of God, nay, we become God Himself, when we cease to believe in our own petty existence, and find that what we call ourselves is but a breath of the universal mind.

But now let us ask Fichte one question. He says that the second stage of life which the universal mind experiences is that of authority. Where does the authority come from? Fichte has told us that nothing can exist outside the universal mind—nay, that besides itself there is no existence at all. Who, then, shall prescribe a limit to this mind? who shall impose an authority upon it? who shall say to it, 'Hitherto shalt thou go, and no farther?' If it be solitary, there must be none to oppose it; if it be boundless, there must be no limit to circumscribe it. These are mere truisms, and yet in the very face of them Fichte has dared to run. He has ventured to conceive a mind which at one and the same moment is independent, yet subject to authority; alone, yet circumscribed; free, yet impeded by an obstacle; unbounded, yet contending with restraint. How can these contradictions be reconciled? how can perfection be made consistent with imperfection? Such is the question we would put to Fichte; such is the question which, we are convinced, Fichte put to himself. It is an undeniable fact that in his later years he abandoned as untenable great part of that ground which he had occupied with such exuberant confidence. It is an undeniable fact that he was more and more driven to admit the real existence of individual limitations, that more and more he was constrained to allow to Man a life in some sense distinct from the universal mind, even though that distinction might be no greater than the difference between the ocean and its waves. But before Fichte had arrived at this stage, the atmosphere of Germany had already been permeated with the breath of a new life; anarchy had passed away, and reconstruction had begun. If Fichte was constrained to modify his views, he was in this rather the follower than the leader of his times; for the age had grown weary with its own waywardness, and was longing for some place of anchorage and rest. Fichte was borne down the stream of public opinion, and, sharing himself in the dissatisfaction with dissolution and anarchy, he struggled to adapt himself to the requirements of an era which was groaning and travailing in spirit. Yet it is not to Fichte that the work of reconstruction belongs. If latterly he embraced that work, he only attached himself to a labour which others had begun; his own mission was to illustrate the last results of unbelief, and when he had exhibited the goal of destruction, his work was done.

And yet we cannot part with Fichte without a word of sympathy. We have said that his unbelief proceeded rather from the despair of arriving at knowledge than from any voluntary choice of his own nature. And our reason for thinking so is this: the man was infinitely superior to his creed. There lived not, there breathed not a nobler spirit than that of Fichte; none more unselfish, none further removed from debasing influences. The man who in his philosophy affects to disparage individual interests, was of all others most eager for the welfare of his fellow-creatures. He who in 1813, amidst the upheaving of the German nations and the outburst of reviving patriotism against French oppression, could go forth to the field of battle, not to fight, but to minister,—he who could forget the interests of personal comfort in his zeal to succour the sick and wounded, and who by the hand of the pestilence could meet a heroic death, a martyr to his own unselfish devotion, is worthy to live in memory when his system of philosophy shall have crumbled in the dust, and shall stand as an eternal monument of that eternal truth, that man is greater than his opinions and larger than the formula of his faith.

CHAPTER VII.

INTRODUCTION TO THE THEOLOGY OF HEGEL AND SCHELLING.

WE are now approaching that which is by far the most difficult portion of German theology, and which is certainly farthest removed from the standpoint of English thought. It cannot be denied that we approach it with something of that satisfaction which a storm-tost mariner feels when for the first time land breaks upon his view. We do not say that we have reached the ultimate boundary of our voyage, we do not say that the land which appears is one flowing with milk and honey—it may prove to be little better than a barren rock; but for all that, it for a time is welcome, as it is a temporary resting-place for the eye amidst the waste of waters. The theology of Hegel and Schelling exhibits certainly a step in the direction of reconstruction, and therefore must in any light be regarded as an advance upon previous systems.

We have thought it right to introduce this subject by a few prefatory remarks, in order that we may reconnoitre the land previous to disembarking. The first and most obvious of these is, that while this theology is in advance of the previous negative system, it is at the same time an evolution from it; it grew out of the very anarchy which it was designed to counteract. Kant had laboured to prove, that when the logical understanding attempts to demonstrate spiritual truth, it is landed in paradoxes and contradictions. This new theology began where Kant ended. It admitted that every truth of the understanding involves a paradox, but it held that paradox is the very essence of truth itself. It announced that there can be no idea which is not the product of contradictions, and that everything in the universe would remain eternally unknown unless its being were revealed by the existence of its opposite. It showed that life could have no existence as an idea unless contrasted with death; that freedom could have no place in the thought unless opposed to slavery; that goodness itself would be a mere state of natural beauty, like the spontaneous bloom of a flower, unless the struggle with evil expanded innocence into virtue. Nor alone did this theology grow out of the contradictions of Kant; it came forth also from the negative standpoint of Fichte. Fichte had said, there is nothing in the universe but mind. This theology answered, Be it so; let us not assume that there is anything more than mind, let us not even assume that there is any other mind than one; out of this one solitary thought I will construct the universe anew, will rediscover all that I have lost—God, Christ, Immortality, and the laws of eternal being. This was the object proposed by the theology of Hegel and Schelling. It took its stand on the threshold of Fichte's system. It stationed itself amidst the ruins, and began to reconstruct them, to unite stone by stone the elements of the temple of truth, to raise from the depths of negation and anarchy a structure which Rationalism could not destroy, whose foundation was fixed in the intuitions of the spirit, and which must endure as long as these intuitions commanded the assent of mankind.

The second thing to be remarked is, that the theology of Hegel and Schelling is one theology. These men are commonly regarded as the founders of separate systems, but it is, we believe, the wildest delusion to suppose that there is any real distinction between them. In the literature of the subject, the system of Schelling is called objective, and that of Hegel absolute idealism. But this distinction is one not of matter, but of form; and when translated into English thought, it means no more than this: Schelling sees the divine plan, and describes it as if he saw it; Hegel feels it in himself, and describes it as if he felt it. Both are engaged in delineating the same idea, but Schelling delineates it in the language of poetry, Hegel in the words of sober prose. It will never be known to which of them the honour is due of having originated the system. Schelling was first on the field, and gave expression to this theology at an earlier stage than Hegel; but there is not wanting some evidence to show that Hegel was the first to suggest what Schelling was the earliest in expressing. It is of the less consequence to determine this point, as the leading idea of their theology is not peculiar to either of them; its novelty lies in its application. The belief that all truth consists in the union of contradictory statements will be found breaking out into occasional flashes at every period of the world's history, even the darkest. It will be found in the philosophic interpretations of Brahminism, in the system of Plato, in the doctrines of Gnosticism, in the belief of the Alexandrian Church, in the theology of Scotus Erigena, in the mysticism of Eckart and Paracelsus, and in the theosophy of Jacob Böhme, Osiander, and Oetinger. There is, therefore, no ground for a charge of plagiarism. Hegel and Schelling, like all other great men, probably only led because they followed; they did not originate that atmosphere which they exhaled. If we were told that Schelling and Hegel, without collusion and without previous intercourse, had at one and the same time given forth to the world a system in all respects identical, we should not be surprised at the fact; we should think it perfectly natural, and should be inclined to judge all the more favourably of their theory. Whatever be the explanation, it is an undeniable truth that the theology of Schelling and Hegel is one and the same.[1] Their language is entirely different; they call the same thing by diverse names; what one terms thought, the other designates the absolute; what one finds first in the soul,

[1] See supplementary note, page 195.

the other begins to look for in nature. But while they speak in different tongues, they give utterance to the same truth; and as we do not intend to adopt the language of either, it shall be our object to exhibit that truth which makes them one.

But before entering upon this subject, it shall be well that we divest ourselves of all prejudice. Let us not come to it with any foregone conclusion; let us not say that we are Hegelians or Anti-Hegelians. Before we are in a position to set ourselves in antagonism to any man's belief, we must be quite sure that we have really understood him—that he means that which we have taken him to mean. Now it so happens that the interpretations of Hegel are as numerous as those of the Bible. We find one writer describing him in these words: 'An infidel, who denied the Personality of God, the personality of man, and the immortality of the soul.' How stands the case? Hegel is so full of God, that he may be called, like Spinoza, 'A God-intoxicated man;' his God is so Personal, that He is Personality itself; and as for the immortality of the soul, it is with Hegel so real, that eternal life is to him not so much a future possession as a present possibility.[1] We find another writer gravely assuring us that Hegel held Absolute Being to be equal to nothing, and that therefore God is with him equal to nonentity. How stands the case? Hegel's conception of God is not that of Absolute Being at all, which, being a mere abstraction, would indeed be equal to nonentity; the

[1] See supplementary note, page 200.

Hegel and Schelling's Theology. 87

God of Hegel is an All-embracing and Self-conscious Personality. We find a third writer still actually starting a preliminary prejudice to the system of Hegel and Schelling on the ground that their ideas will be found in the heart of Gnosticism and Platonism; forgetting that the want of originality, while it detracts from the merit of the author, adds to the truth of his utterance: the oldest thoughts are probably the most real. Our design in noticing these things is far removed from special pleading; we speak purely in the interest of candour and fairness. It is a principle of jurisprudence, it is a principle even of common morality, that we should believe a man to speak the truth until we have good reason to suspect his veracity. Now it is an indisputable fact that Hegel died in the communion of the Lutheran Church, and that he professed to be a sincere believer in the Christian religion. In these circumstances it is only right, it is only reasonable, it is only a point of simple justice, that we should assign to him the name which he claimed for himself, unless we have fair grounds for questioning his legitimate title to it. If we have not studied his writings, if we ourselves have had no personal intercourse with the mind of the man, it will not do for us, on the authority of detached sentences quoted by others, to pronounce him an infidel, a denier of Divine Personality, and a proclaimer of the belief that God is equal to nothing. We are all more or less swayed by deference to great names, but in this case we must dismiss all deference which is not founded upon the personal knowledge of a writer with his subject. We have a perfect right to accept or to reject the opinion of any author; but let us beware that we know that opinion, that we have heard the voice itself and not merely the echo of the voice. By his own words a man may be justified or condemned, but not by the interpretation of these words which others may choose to put upon them. For our part, we intend to view this subject impartially, to judge the system by itself alone. We do not say that we have no preliminary bias; we do not know that it is possible to approach any subject without such a bias. But in this case our bias arises from the fact that Hegel has declared himself to be a Christian, and from respect to the legal principle that a man should be considered true until he has been proved to have spoken falsely. This, and nothing else than this, is the feeling of favour with which we approach the Hegelian Theology. Hegel announced himself to be a Lutheran; and we shall assume that his system is in accordance with his profession until we are driven to abandon this position by the testimony of the system itself.

There is one other remark which we would premise before introducing this theology to the student. We have said that the theology of Schelling and Hegel is identical; yet it must have struck the student that throughout this chapter we have associated it chiefly with the name of the latter. The practice, indeed, is a universal one; we never call a man of this school a Schellingian, but always a Hegelian. Nor is it difficult to perceive the reason of this. Schelling and Hegel are indeed identical in idea, but they are vastly different in the degree of their perfection. If Schelling is the originator, Hegel is certainly the finisher of the work; and we judge a system not by its earliest, but by its latest manifestation. Schelling may be the bud, the germ, the beginning; but Hegel is the full-blown flower. Schelling looked out upon the world, surveyed it with the eye of a poet, and found in it the presence of a Trinity, whose operation he traced down to the human soul itself; Hegel entered into the recesses of his own spirit, studied in its minutest details the working of the human heart, and found in it a God, whose operation he traced to the world. Schelling began with the superstructure, and ended with the foundation; Hegel commenced with the foundation, and reared upon it the superstructure. And the strength of their personal convictions corresponded to their relative standpoints. Schelling had no settled opinion; Schwegler says that he changed his mind five times. This, at least, is certain, that he abandoned at the last the very essence of the Hegelian Theology. But Hegel was consistent throughout. There is no trace of the slightest wavering in his system. When he had embraced it, he adhered to it; extending it, no doubt, into ever widening applications, yet never essentially changing or even modifying its principles. On this account it is that, both in his own and succeeding times, he has been placed at the head of that school which he contributed so largely to rear.

Although not the first to institute it nor the last to embrace it, he is yet the man who, of all others, has done the most to render it perpetual; and therefore posterity has unanimously agreed that the theology which owes to him its highest elaboration shall in future be called by his name.

CHAPTER VIII.

TRINITY OF SCHELLING AND HEGEL.

WE will now attempt an explanation of this very difficult subject—difficult chiefly from that region of abstraction which must be traversed in order to explore it. The great object to be effected is the bridging over of that gulf which intervenes between German and English thought. The abstract is naturally a foreign land to the British mind; it has long been accustomed to dwell rather amongst things than thoughts; and it is on this ground, and on this ground alone, that the charge of mysticism has been so often preferred against the Hegelian Theology. We shall therefore make it our aim as far as possible to disregard the terminology of Hegel and Schelling, and to consider purely the translation of their ideas into our own mode of thinking; in this way we shall be enabled to exhibit them in one view, for it is only their language that constitutes their difference. The leading point in the theology of Hegel and Schelling is the idea of the Trinity. In other theological creeds, the Trinity is held as one of the doctrines; but here it forms the entire system, it is the theology itself. And now, on the very threshold of the subject, we are met by a difference between English and German thought. To our mode of thinking, the most elementary idea in the world is that of unity. The Hegelian says this is a mistake; he affirms that the simplest idea is not a unity, but a trinity. The student must grasp this at the outset, for it is at once the foundation and key to the whole system. It is the doctrine of Hegel and Schelling that every thought in the human mind is made up of three elements, two of which are contradictory, and the third a uniting link which reconciles them. Take, they say, the most elementary idea which you possess, and you will find in your own experience that it is not elementary at all, but a compound of contradictions. What, for example, is that thought which lies beneath all other thoughts ? Is it not self-consciousness ? Surely, if unity be found anywhere, it must be here ; for can anything be less complex than the idea of your own existence ? And yet, if we examine the matter more closely, we shall find that self-consciousness is not a single idea, but the union of two distinct and even contrary ideas,—self and non-self. Take away either of these, and self-consciousness must vanish. Suppose, for a moment, that there were no object in the world except your individual self; the very supposition is almost impossible, but we will try to imagine it. Conceive, if you can, that you had entered into a life in which there was no other but you, and no other part even of you except a soul— no external world, no brother man, no outward body, nothing to see, or hear, or handle; only life. It is manifest that, in these circumstances, you would never come to know that you were a living being. When you say, *I* think, *I* speak, *I* believe, you speak of yourself as distinguished from some other person, you mark yourself out as a distinct personality standing apart from other men; but in the very act of doing so you assume the existence of other men. We only come to know ourselves by knowing that there is something not ourselves, and without that knowledge we would remain for ever unconscious of our own being; we would be living but with a life equal to death. That is the reason why Hegel says that absolute being would be equal to nothing, meaning clearly that perfect self-seclusion would deprive us even of our own self-consciousness. Here, then, we have reached the foundation-stone of the Hegelian system. The most fundamental thought in the human mind is the idea of self-consciousness. This thought, although fundamental, is yet complex; it is made up of the union of two ideas, —self and non-self. The human mind, therefore, has a trinity within itself; its very existence is tri-une. The essence of spirit is self-consciousness, and self-consciousness is the blending together in one thought of the world within and the world without, the visible and the invisible, the thinking being who says *I*, and the unthinking object which calls forth his thought: Man is a trinity.

We believe that thus far no one will impugn the system of Hegel and Schelling. Whatever may or may not be true in their later speculations, the fact from which they start is at least unquestionable, and that is the assertion that the very act of thinking involves a trinity of thought. Before we advance farther, let the student be firmly persuaded that he has grasped this point; if he has not, the sequel must be utterly unintelligible to him, for in this system other foundation can no man lay. Let us try to put the matter a little more popularly. Instead of self-consciousness, let us use a word which means the same thing, personality. What is a person? It is not a soul; it is not a body; it is a union of both. A body without a soul is a corpse; a soul without a body would be equal to a corpse, for it would remain unconscious of itself; but when the two meet together they constitute a person, a living being, a man. Here is a very simple statement of that foundation on which is built the most elaborate system of theology which has ever been conceived, so simple that he who runs may read. It is a matter of experience; we have only to look within, and we feel it, see it, know it to be true. All human beings call themselves persons; and all mean by personality the possession of a soul and a body, the union of two things which, when considered separately, have opposite attributes—the blending of a world which is invisible with a world which is seen and temporal. We repeat, then, that thus far the common sense of mankind is at one with Hegel and Schelling; all must concede that there is a trinity in human thought. But are we prepared with them to take the next step,—to say that what exists in Man exists also in God? Perhaps a preliminary question should be, Have we any right to take it? Have we any reason to assume, that because we have received a certain mental constitution, the same mental constitution will be found in the Author of the universe? In making such an assumption, do we not desert the firm ground of logic, and build our edifice upon the shifting sand? Now we have promised to consider this theology impartially, and therefore we have no wish to overstate facts. We concede at once that to transfer the laws of human thought to God is an assumption— an assumption not only unproved, but incapable of proof. We hold, nevertheless, that such an assumption is necessary; every theology, nay, every science must assume something to be true. Theology, before advancing a step, must take it for granted that Man is made in the image of God. There can be no theology where there has not previously been a religion, and the foundation of every religious system must be laid in the heart. On this ground we think that Hegel and Schelling have not transgressed the limits of theological science in assuming that what exists in Man must have its ground in the Absolute Mind. In doing so they certainly deprive their system of mathematical certainty, but they nowhere claim to rest it on mathematical certainty. Schelling founds it upon an intellectual intuition; Hegel, on the revelation of God within the soul. We need not, therefore, blame them because their system does not exhibit that logical precision which they never intended it to possess. Their theology, like every science, is built upon a conviction which cannot be proved, only in their case it is not an axiom of the intellect, but a sentiment of the heart; it is the belief that the mind of man is constructed after the image of God.

Let us, then, advance with Hegel and Schelling to their next step. They have already shown that what we call the human spirit is a trinity comprehending the union of two ideas, self and non-self—in other words, a soul and a body. They now proceed to transfer the process from the human to the divine. What is true of the spirit of Man is true, they say, of the Spirit of God. That Divine Spirit which we call the Third Person of the Trinity is in one sense the first, for it is the very Personality of God. A human spirit or person is the union of a soul and a body; even so the Divine Spirit or Personality must be the union of a soul and a body. It must embrace within itself both the Father and the Son,—the Father corresponding to the universal soul, the Son being that body or house which constitutes the dwelling-place of that soul. The Father could never at any time have been alone. To suppose that at any period the Father dwelt alone would be to imagine a God unconscious of His own existence, because, without an object of thought, it would be a soul without a body. Therefore, from all eternity, the Infinite Being must have possessed a dwelling-place, a house not made with hands, eternal in the heavens; and that house must have been another self, an image of His own glory, a mirror in which the Father could behold Himself reflected—in a word, it must have been at once separate from the Father and yet a part of His very being, just as the human body is separate from the soul and yet a part of its being. Christ is the house of God. He is the image of the Infinite Spirit, the glass by which He sees Himself, the body which forms the outward side of His Personality. As the Son was afterwards incarnate in the human soul, so it may be said that from all eternity the Father was incarnate in the Son; for He was the place of His habitation, the home of His rest, the embodiment of His thought, the realization of His existence—in a word, what the sacred writer calls Him, the brightness of His glory and the express image of His person.

We have interpreted the Hegelian Trinity evangelically. In so doing, we are quite aware that we will incur the criticism of a great part of the Hegelians and the whole of the non-Hegelians. It has of late years been accepted as an axiom that Hegel believed God to be originally impersonal, and that he regarded Him as for the first time attaining to Personality in the earthly form of the man Christ Jesus. If it be so, then, indeed, in this theology there is no proper Trinity. But let it be remembered that this is not a question of theory, but of fact. We have followed our universal principle of believing a man's word until we have found reason to doubt it; and Hegel declares in explicit terms that the Trinity is independent of time, and existing above the world. That assertion Hegel has nowhere contradicted. We will not say that he has nowhere made statements which seem to be inconsistent with it; we merely contend that they are inconsistencies, and nothing more. There are twenty inconsistent persons for every ten hypocrites—nay, it is our belief that the large majority of those who are charged with hypocrisy have really been guilty only of inconsistency, have erred by defect of the intellect rather than by depravation of the heart. We concede that to this intellectual halting Hegel has on one or two occasions formed no exception. We concede that in the case of Schelling there was at first a strong leaning towards the view of an impersonal God who became a Trinity in the world. We concede that many who profess to be direct followers of Hegel and Schelling have honestly regarded this as the legitimate outcome of their system. But the question is not now what is or is not the legitimate outcome of anything, but simply what is the fact. And is it not a notorious fact that Schelling became ultimately a strenuous defender of the divine Personality? Is it not an indisputable fact that Hegel all along declared his belief in a Trinity above and beyond time? Is it not a matter of history that their two earliest disciples, Daub and Marheinecke, adopted their system as a philosophic defence of Christianity? With these facts before us, we have no recourse but to accept this theology for what it claims to be. Its later developments have, indeed, led to the denial not merely of a personal God, but of any God whatsoever; yet it may be fairly questioned how far these later developments are real and logical inferences from the system on which they profess to build. Whether they be so or not, we shall not be justified in judging of the design of an author by the consequences of his theory. Whatever be the merits or demerits of Schelling and Hegel, they certainly contemplated the establishment of a pure spiritualism, in which the human soul would shine forth in its native immortality; and it never entered into their minds that in the course of another generation their system would be promulgated as a guide to Materialism, and their names handed down as the watchwords of Atheism. These consequences, really or falsely deduced from their speculations, were never foreseen by themselves, and therefore with these consequences they are not in justice chargeable. By their personal design alone they must be judged; and in the absence of any contradictory statement in their writings, their personal design should be gathered without questioning from their own testimony to their object and aim.

But we must now advance again. We have seen that this theology recognises an eternal Trinity, and therefore starts from the conception of a Personal God. But here there opens a great mystery. That which is perfect in eternity appears in time as if it were imperfect. In eternity the Trinity is for ever completed, but in time it is seen like something only coming into completeness—is represented not as a finished idea, but as a long-protracted process, in which God seems for a time to lose His other self, and only to find Him after many days. We know even in this world how the conception of a great artist may be perfect in idea before it is placed on the canvas. We know, also, that whenever it begins to be placed on the canvas, the perfection appears to vanish. The idea was bright and beautiful in the artist's mind, but when he comes to work it out, it seems as if he could never realize it. The inward creation was reached by a momentary flash, but the outward one, the creation on the canvas, can only be reached through blots and mars and erasures; the first perfection exists at the beginning, but the last is a perfection through suffering. And all this is a feeble type of the Great Artist whose thought is in eternity, but whose canvas is the world of time. In eternity, He possesses a complete personality and all the perfections of an infinite nature, but to imprint these in a moment upon the canvas of time would be a contradiction in terms. Time can only represent things after the order of succession, it cannot show them in the instantaneous flash of eternity. Hence, on the temporal canvas, the Trinity of God is seen gradually unfolding. The Infinite Father is beheld for a time with no other to commune with Him, separated from His creatures, and in search of a resting-place for His love. The creature is beheld for a time separated from the Infinite Father, struggling to support himself in a far country, and at length arriving, through failure, at the conviction that distance is misery. Then comes the reunion, the reconciliation, the meeting again of Heaven and earth, the marriage of the Infinite and finite. In Christ, the perfect Man, God finds His other self, the Universal Soul discovers its embodiment, its house, its resting-place; and in the union between the soul and its embodiment the Trinity is perfected. Such is the course of God in time; such is the divine plan of this universe. The Infinite Spirit loses His life that He may find it again, parts from His other self that He may get Him back through suffering, and regains in the heart of Man that fellowship which He had lost in the deadness of material nature. To the working out of this striking scheme we must address ourselves in the following chapter.

CHAPTER IX.

EVOLUTION OF THE HEGELIAN TRINITY IN TIME.

EVERY soul must embody itself; for a soul without a body would be dead, it would want the half of its personality. The Infinite Soul, the Soul of the universe, must follow the same law; it must find for itself a body, a house, a dwelling-place. The Infinite Soul seeking a body is what we call the act of creation; it is spirit manifesting itself in form. The first embodiment of God is nature—that is, the first embodiment of God in time, for, as we have seen, He has an eternal habitation above time. But in time His earliest house is nature; here first the Infinite Spirit speaks out from its solitude, passes from self-contemplation into outward manifestation. In the beginning God created the heavens and the earth, and He did so to manifest His glory. A soul without a body cannot manifest its glory; its riches would be all self-contained. But the moment it has received a body it ceases to live within itself, it enters into a life beyond its own being. When God created the heavens and the earth, the Soul of the universe found its first temporal embodiment, and came forth from the contemplation of eternity into the activity of time.

But nature, this first temporal embodiment of the Eternal Spirit, was not adequate to express His glory; the body was too contracted to hold the Spirit; it did not furnish the Universal Soul with a countenance eloquent enough to speak forth the depths that slumbered within it. God could, indeed, speak to nature, but nature could not respond to God. The communion was all on one side; and where the communion is on one side, there can be no manifestation of a Trinity. The Trinity can only be manifested where there is a spirit of communion going forth from the Father to a kindred soul, and coming back again from that kindred soul to the Father. But nature was incapable of being the kindred heart of God. It had no answer to give to the voice of the Eternal Father; it had no spirit of communion to send back in response to the message of Infinite Love. Nature was only a recipient, it had nothing to give in return, and therefore it was utterly unable to break the solitude of the Eternal Spirit; unless it could be kindled into a life higher than its own, it must ever have remained separate from the life of God.

But, strange to say, there was in this dead, material nature the possibility of a great kindling—of a life which, although now latent, might ultimately respond to the heart of God. That it should be so we need not wonder, for nature, with all its imperfections, is still the body of God, and we know that the body always shares somewhat in the life of the soul. Accordingly there is in nature, even at its lowest stage, a centre of latent life, the result of its union with the Infinite Spirit. Nor can this life remain for ever latent; by an inevitable necessity of its being, it must expand, and broaden, and grow. It is originally a tiny spark, but it contains within itself a potential fire, which shall yet blaze forth into a life that can respond to God. Not falsely, therefore, is it that poets have described material objects as endowed with life and intelligence; not falsely is it that the man of science has delighted to think of nature as a system of vital forces capable of great possibilities; for in the depth of its being nature is indeed not dead, but alive with that life which the body derives from the soul. Gradually this life of nature unfolds itself. Unconscious in the mineral, it passes in the plant into something like a striving after sentient being, though as yet it is only the life of sleep, hardly distinguishable from the nothingness of death. In the animal it reaches a higher stage; the sleep becomes a dream, and the lethargy is partially broken. At length in the man it wakes; the sleep and the dream alike disappear, and the life of nature becomes a living soul.

And now for the first time there arises a conflict in the universe. We have said that nature was from the very outset a separation from God, inasmuch as the body was too small to express the thoughts of the Infinite Soul. Yet to nature this separation was not a source of pain, because its life was as yet latent, and

it was incapable of feeling. But now, in the spirit of
Man, the life of nature has awakened into conscious
being, and with the consciousness there has come the
pain. Man feels that the life of nature is in him, and
that this life is separation from God. He perceives
for the first time that there is a law in his members
warring against the law of his mind. He realizes that
there is a battle going on within him. On the one
hand there is a will, a conscious personality, which
commands him to rise out of his material limitations,
and to assert his freedom in the universe of God.
But on the other hand there is a lower life within him,
the life of nature, which chains him to the dust, which
tells him he is earth-born and a slave. The personality
of will points him ever out of himself, but nature
encloses him within her own barriers, and forbids him
to transcend the sphere of the body and the sense;
the life of nature is the life of selfishness. It is now
that there wakes in man that terrible unrest which
we call the sense of sin. As long as there was no
personal will, there was no sin; we had not known
sin but for the law. The life which slept in the plant
and dreamed in the animal was essentially a selfish
life, yet in these selfishness was not sin; it is the
nature of a plant and of an animal to keep within
themselves. But in Man there was a compound life.
He received by inheritance the nature both of the
vegetable and of the animal world; but in addition to
that he received something more—a personal will,
which impelled him to pass out of himself, and urged

him to transcend his limits. It was not a sin in the plant to be a plant, it was not a sin in the animal to be an animal; but to be either the one or the other was a sin in Man. Man, indeed, retained the nature of both; but it was only as a survival of the past, as a memory of former days. There had been breathed into him the breath of a higher life, and it was this higher life which made him Man. To follow the existence of the plant or of the animal was in him treason against the law of his being, self-degradation— in a word, sin. And therefore it was that with Man for the first time there arose a struggle; therefore it was that in him there woke the earliest sense of separation from the life of God, that unrest which is in itself so painful, and yet without which there can be no return. 'The man is become as one of us, to know good and evil;' such is the language in which the awakening is described. The conflict of will with nature brought the knowledge of sin, and the knowledge of sin brought the sense of separation.

Now, just in proportion as Man feels the sense of separation from God, there will be felt the longing to return, and the longing to return will be deepest when the separation is realized as complete. There is nothing paradoxical in this; it is just as true in religion as it is in philosophy. An absolutely bad man would have no sense of separation from God; the feeling of separation is really the beginning of the return, the first stage in the process of conversion. Accordingly, Man was never in so favourable a position for the reception of a new life as at that moment when he felt the utmost extent of his isolation from the heart of God. That was the fulness of the time, it was the extremity of human helplessness; and Man's extremity was God's opportunity. In this respect the theology of Hegel and Schelling coincides with the dictates of the most evangelical orthodoxy; thus far, indeed, they might without hypocrisy, and with scarcely a mental reservation, have signed the Thirty-nine Articles or the Westminster Confession. In what follows, however, there is more difficulty in arriving at a clear statement of their views.

Man, we have seen, longs for a return; but what good is there in the longing? A mere desire will not effect its object. The spirit of Man may be willing to go back to God, but the flesh is not only weak, but contrary, and before he can return the flesh must be crucified. Can this barrier be removed by Man himself? Can humanity out of its own depths bring forth a being who will succeed in liberating the human race from the thraldom of nature, and in restoring it to the glorious liberty of the sons of God? It is generally held by the opponents of this theology that Hegel and Schelling concede such a power to the unaided strength of Man. If so, then, indeed, their system can no longer claim to be an exposition of Christianity, for if humanity can bring forth its Redeemer out of itself, there is no need to look for the supernatural in the Christ of the gospel; nor, if we allow such a power to our own unaided nature, does there seem to be any necessity for redemption at all.

But is this really the view of Schelling and Hegel? Let us quote the authority of one who, while he belongs to this school, will not be suspected of any undue partiality for the historical truth of the gospel; we mean Rosencranz. Rosencranz says, in so many words, that the life latent in nature has power at special times specially to exert itself, and he considers the appearance of the God-man to have been pre-eminently one of those seasons. Let us quote the authority of another, who is said to have baptized Hegel into Christ, but who really thought that he had found Christ in Hegel; we mean Rothe. Rothe distinctly states his conviction that the life of the body is presided over by the life of the soul; in other words, that nature at every new stage of its development involves the exercise of a supernatural power. We ought to remember, also, that in the Hegelian Theology the world effects nothing by itself; the world apart from the Universal Spirit is a mere negation, and at no time can it be anything higher than the finite medium through which the Universal Spirit reveals Himself. Accordingly, we are unable to resist the conclusion that this theology requires a supernatural Redeemer. He must, indeed, be in the world; He must come forth from the midst of the world; He must even manifest Himself when the world has reached the utmost extremity of its earthliness. Nevertheless, that world must be rather the occasion than the cause of His existence; He must be born from above. At the last stage of helplessness, we must conceive the impartation of a new, a divine assistance, of a supernatural force added to the life of nature, by which it brings into being a perfect Man—a Man who, while He is linked with all that have gone before Him, and associated with all that stand beside Him, shall yet perceive His affinity with One who is higher than these, even with the Infinite Father Himself, and who shall struggle to bring back that humanity, of which He is the climax and the crown, into fellowship and reunion with the God from whom it is separated. Such must be the Redeemer of the world; such must be the work which is given Him to do. Between Man and the heart of the Father there is a great gulf fixed; and that gulf is the life of nature, which is another name for the life of selfishness. The Redeemer of the world, if He would restore communion between earth and heaven, must root out from humanity this nature-life, this self-love, this search for individual happiness, which keeps the soul imprisoned within the narrow precincts of the world, and prevents it from soaring upward and onward. This was the redemption, this was the emancipation which the gospel effected; this was the restoration of the creature into the glorious liberty of the sons of God. The entire life of the Redeemer, beginning with the manger and culminating with the cross, was a crucifixion of individual happiness, a life-sermon illustrating the words, 'Not my will, but Thine be done.' His whole being was the search for life through death; the casting of the corn, of wheat into the ground, that it might not abide alone. Hitherto humanity had been abiding alone. Instead of finding its being in the sense of brotherhood, it had divided itself into antagonistic individual elements, perpetually at war with one another, and each seeking to subsist independently of the other; this was the life of nature, the life of selfishness. The perfect Man broke the chain, and set the prisoners free. He crucified the life of nature, and thereby destroyed the wall of partition which separated every man from his brother, and in so doing separated him from God. He bridged over the gulf of nature by love. He destroyed that which had led each man to conceive himself as an isolated unit, as an individual whose life lay apart from all other lives, apart even from the life of God. In breaking down the barrier of nature and selfishness, He restored at once the communion of man with man and the communion of Man with God, united humanity into one grand brotherhood, and lifted it up right into the presence of the Infinite Father. Heaven and earth met together; God and Man were reconciled, and the completed Trinity was revealed. In one Spirit of Personality the Father and the Son were united; the soul had found a body, and the body had found a soul. The life which the Infinite Father had given to nature was given back by nature in richer, nobler form, and the bread which He had cast upon the waters was found again after many days; for in the Spirit of the perfect Son of man He reached again His native dwelling-place, the house not made with hands, eternal in the heavens.

CHAPTER X.

EVOLUTION OF THE HEGELIAN TRINITY IN THE HISTORY OF THE CHURCH.

THE self-surrender of the Son of man was completed by His death, for in this was perfectly accomplished the crucifixion of the individual nature. Hegel says that the death of Christ was the crowning proof at once of His humanity and of His divinity. It was the proof of His humanity because it revealed Him in the utmost extremity of weakness, and at the same time it was the surest road to the revelation of His Deity, because it removed that visible presence which had been the greatest hindrance to its acceptance. It is the distinct doctrine of Hegel, that as long as Christ was manifest in the flesh, the very manifestation constituted a veil which concealed His perfect divinity from the eyes of men; hence the Redeemer looks forward to His death as His true exaltation. 'It is expedient for you that I go away;' 'I, if I be lifted up from the earth, will draw all men unto me.' The death of Christ was the portal to His resurrection into a higher life,—a life no longer limited to one particular spot of earth, no longer confined to one special tribe or nation, or family, but world-wide, universal, cosmopolitan, all-embracing in its influence, and rendering Him no more the Son of David, but exclusively the Son of man.

This resurrection-life of Christ is manifested in the Church; here is the meeting-point between the theology of Hegel and that of Schleiermacher. In the life of the Christian Church the Son of man repeats Himself, passes through the same stages of development which marked His historical appearance, grows in wisdom and in knowledge, and unfolds new perfections as the ages roll; until at last He shall reach, in the collective souls of His followers, that divine height which He exhibited in His own individual history, even the measure of the stature of the perfect Man. Accordingly, we must expect to find in the life of the Church of God a real law of progress, a genuine principle of growth, by which, without any possibility of accident or chance or contingency, it shall pass from stage to stage, and gain at each new epoch that strength which was wanting to the old. In a word, if we have grasped that principle of development which has been already revealed in the evolution of the Trinity in time, we have attained to a predictive power, by which we can not only observe the providence of passing events, but are able ourselves to prophesy what these events must be. If we have arrived at this, we shall no longer look with despondency upon the seeming anarchy which in many places the Church reveals; for we shall see that these apparent blemishes are in reality necessary stages in our life, the shades which bring out her light, the minor notes which, in themselves discordant, are in their union with the whole the highest harmony. To the exhibition of this law of progress we now briefly address ourselves.

We have seen that there are three things which constitute divine Personality,—a body, a soul, and the union between them. In the life of the Church the divine Personality repeats itself, and therefore here also we must be prepared to find three stages of existence. In the actual life of God the body and the soul are eternally united; but in the Church there is no eternal union, but only a union after many days. The history of the Church exhibits the following progressive periods: There is, first, that period in which the body has the pre-eminence over the soul, in which the external and historical and sensational are stronger than the inward and spiritual; there is, secondly, that epoch in which the soul predominates over the body, in which Man begins to assert his individuality, and claims the privilege of private thought and self-reflection; there is, thirdly, that age in which the soul and the body are reconciled, in which reason ceases to revolt against historical authority, and the human intellect finds a point of union with the facts of revelation. These three stages are actually exhibited in the history of the Christian world; but before attempting to illustrate them, the student may as well look nearer home, and see how they are exhibited in his own individual life. Every man is an epitome of all history; every man has the same three stages in his earthly existence. Individual life begins with the experience of outward sensations, and amidst these sensations its earliest years are passed. The body has in these days a pre-eminence over the soul, and we are more eager to observe than to reflect upon our observations. In that transition period when youth begins to melt into manhood, there comes a reaction against this state of things; the soul asserts its superiority to the body, and refuses any longer to be subject to authority; the reign of sensation has been succeeded by the empire of reflection. Now both of these stages, if carried to an extreme, are dangerous. The predominance of the body over the soul is the conquest of Man's rational nature by his animal instincts, and therefore, when he succumbs to this condition, he resigns his birthright, and becomes as the beast of the field. The predominance of the soul over the body must lead either to scepticism or to mysticism, for in each of these phases the mind rejects all outward authority, and constitutes itself the arbiter of truth; hence the period of reflection is generally the epoch of heresies. But with mature and completed manhood there comes a third stage, reconciling the other two; it is the union of the body and the soul, the balance of reason and authority, the perfect equilibrium between the sense and the spirit: this is the age of calmness, of sobriety, of peace. Such are the three periods of individual life. We require no history to verify them, but, on the contrary, we take them to verify history; their existence is bound up in our own existence. Let us now see how this individual life is paralleled in outward history.

The history of the Church begins with the external, the outward, the historical—in a word, with the life of the body; and this period extends from the first Christian century to the time of the Reformation. It may be called the Judaism of Christianity. Men are here not so much concerned with the essence of life as with its form, not so much with religion itself as with the ceremonies in which it is clothed, not so much with the principles of Christianity as with the outward historical facts which express these principles. The sacraments are here not only the source of life, but themselves the very life of the soul. Regeneration is the result of a dynamical process,—we had almost said a material process,—in which the spirit of Man is entirely passive. The scenes of Christ's life are of more interest than the life itself, and the world looks back with a superstitious veneration to the sacred sepulchre and the holy city. To recover these out of the hands of the infidels is regarded as the most religious work which can await the mind of Man, and he who attaches himself to that work has a sure passport to the favour of Heaven. All Europe embarks in the enterprise. Great armies go forth, animated by an enthusiasm which they mistake for religion, but which is in reality only a sensuous heroism. They are for a time successful, their arms are crowned with triumph, the sepulchre and the city and all their hallowed associations are rescued from the Mahommedans. But the golden age is not yet; religion is as far off as ever. It could not be otherwise. These men, like the women of old, were seeking the dead body of Jesus, with this distinction, that while the women believed their Saviour to be dead, and rejoiced to find Him alive, the crusaders believed Him to be alive, but were intent on finding His body: they sought a dead Christ, and would have been but indifferently pleased to find a living one; they were more anxious to garnish His sepulchre than to reproduce His life. And then in this sensuous religion there was something, if possible, more destructive to spirituality still. There was no such thing as belief in the truth; there was only belief in the authority that proclaimed it, and unfortunately that authority was external to the soul: it was a collective visible organism, the outward Church. Individual impressions were nothing, private thought on any subject relating to religion was a mark of heresy and schism, the outward voice of the Church was paramount and supreme, and nothing was left for the individual mind but to become recipient of the doctrines which it promulgated. Such a state of things could not last; for the soul has a birthright, and it must sooner or later assert it. Not even in the days of Papal supremacy could the reaction be altogether suppressed; it burst out from time to time, and though repeatedly extinguished, was powerful by the prophecy which it gave of its infinite possibilities. At last the fulness of the time came, and the human spirit broke its fetters. The Reformation was the reaction of the soul against the domination of the body, the assertion of individual right against the unity of the Church. Man refused any longer to be a piece of mechanism, and claimed the prerogative of a thinking being. Such a reaction was inevitable; it had only waited its time, and it came just at the right time. If it had come sooner, it would have been premature, and therefore unsuccessful,— would have shared the fate of the Paulicians, of the Waldenses, of Jerome, and Huss, and Savonarola. This system of Church-domination, which was an evil at the time of the Reformation, was a supreme good during the Dark Ages; it was that state of tutelage which St. Paul calls the schoolmaster, who prepares the way for the intelligent reception of Christian truth. Accordingly, the Reformation was not a day too late; it was the right movement in the right place, and just because it was opportune in its occurrence, it was profoundly beneficial in its effects.

Yet this reaction, just because it was a reaction, was not free from liability to abuse, and, in point of fact, it was not long in being subjected to that abuse. The soul was not content with liberating itself from the domination of the body, it sought ere long to shake off the body altogether; and that movement, which began with a tendency to reformation, ended in a system of pure negation—the anarchy of Rationalism. As the Church of the Middle Ages had exhibited the attempt of the body to exist without the soul, so the speculations of the eighteenth century exhibit the attempt of the soul to exist without the body. Accordingly, it is evident that there must be a third stage, in which the extreme Catholic and the extreme Protestant principles will be reconciled in a harmonious unity, in which the body shall accept its position as subordinate to the soul, and the soul shall be content to acknowledge the necessity of the body. Has this third period of peace and concord yet dawned upon the world? Hegel, Schelling, and the Germans in general affirm that it has, and they consider the Hegelian Theology to be its representative and its illustration. Schelling says that the first age was that of Peter, and extended to the Reformation; that the second was that of Paul, which began with the revolt from legalism, and ended with the elevation of human reason over all systems of truth; and that the third and brightest age is that of John,— the reconciling power of love, which brings harmony out of discord, and unites the conflicting elements into a great calm: this, he says, has come with German transcendentalism. We suppose it is not unnatural for every nation to consider itself the acme of human development; for Germany it can at least be said, that she has made an honest attempt to realize the period of Johannine reconciliation. That she has succeeded, that any nation has succeeded in such an aim, we cannot, with a view of the existing world, for a moment believe. But if this period of reconciliation has not yet been reached, it by no means affects the philosophic truth of those laws of history which German transcendentalism has exhibited. That history begins with the external, passes into the subjective or internal,

in the History of the Church.

and culminates with the reconciliation of both, is a principle which can be verified by every department of human study. It is the glory of the transcendental system that it claims for theology the position of a real progressive science, that it has succeeded in some measure in tracing the footsteps of the Infinite Spirit through the course of time, and that it has arrived, however faintly and imperfectly, yet truly, at the exhibition of a great world-plan, towards the consummation of which the whole creation moves. These are its bright features, and these we shall not deny it. Yet this transcendental theology is susceptible of a darker shade,—a shade which, we believe, entered not into the picture of Hegel himself, but which has certainly obtained the numerical victory in the minds of his followers. To the exhibition of this dark side in the system we must now briefly direct our attention, for it has coloured all the speculations of Germany for the last forty years, and has gone far to identify the spiritualism of the transcendental theology with the fatalistic materialism which professed to be its opposite extreme.

CHAPTER XI.

THE RIGHT AND THE LEFT.

WE have said that the Hegelian Theology has been subjected to a multitude of interpretations. These diversities, however, have been summed up under two general divisions, which have been called respectively the Right and the Left. The theologians who belong to the Right represent the orthodox party; those who adopt the Left are opposed to historical Christianity. We intend to offer the student a brief explanation of the views of these parties. Of all parts of the transcendental theology, it is perhaps the most difficult to make clear to the English mind; but we shall endeavour, as much as possible, to divest it of that abstract character which constitutes its mysticism, and to clothe it in such language as will render it intelligible. We have seen that, according to the Hegelian Theology, the Personality of God must be a Trinity, because personality always implies a soul, a body, and the union of these in one being. We have seen that the Soul of the universe would have remained eternally unconscious of His own life unless from all eternity He had possessed an embodiment by which

The Right and the Left.

He recognised Himself in contrast to something which was not Himself—just as the individual mind never could employ the expressions, '*I* think,' '*I* speak,' '*I* believe,' unless it had first received the idea of something other than itself; it only uses the word *I* in antithesis to some other being. It is the body which distinguishes one soul from another, and which enables each soul to recognise itself as separate from the others; for it is the body that walls in the soul from all beside, and so constitutes the partition-line of each man's individual nature. It is assumed, then, as a first principle, alike by the Right and the Left, that in order to contemplate God as a Person we must think of Him as a Trinity, that is, as the union of a soul and a body. But the point of divergence between the Right and the Left lies in the answer to the question, 'What is the body of God? what is the dwelling-place of the Infinite soul?' It is the opinion of the Right that the dwelling-place of the Father, the perfect embodiment of the Divine Spirit, is the Son of man; that in Him dwelt all the fulness of the Godhead bodily. This is the view which in the last few chapters we have been endeavouring to expound. We have accepted the Right as the ultimate opinion of Schelling and the exclusive opinion of Hegel; and we are confirmed in this by the fact, that when Hegel first gave his system to the world, it was received not as an off-shoot of scepticism, but as a defence of Christianity.[1] Yet since the days of Hegel an attempt has been made to show that his system

[1] See supplementary note, page 203.

legitimately leads to the opposite conclusion ; and this step has been taken by the interpreters of the Left. The Hegelians of the Left deny that the Divine Spirit can ever be embodied in an individual form. Such an embodiment, they say, would be a contradiction in terms. The Spirit of the universe is infinite, an individual body is finite; for God, therefore, to be manifested in an individual would be the embodiment of an infinite being in a finite form—in other words, the limiting of that which is by nature unlimited. According to this philosophy, the Infinite Spirit can only be represented in the entire race of completed humanity. God cannot dwell in any man; He can only find His abode in human nature as a whole. It follows from this that as yet the Infinite Spirit has never found a body, and therefore has not yet arrived at Personality; He is only becoming Personal—is, as the world advances, gradually awakening into the recognition of Himself, and will only perfectly recognise Himself when the last individual of the human series shall stand upon the earth. Now let the student distinctly realize this position of the Left; let him measure its consequences, even while he avoids imputing these consequences to the intention of its adherents. For if we mistake not, this theory is in advance of Atheism itself. Atheism merely says there is no God; the Left Hegelianism says there is a God, but we are creating Him. In this theology it is Man that gives Personality to the Infinite Spirit; each individual of the race is helping to make Him conscious of His own existence, and the last individual of all will have the merit of completing the process. God is here the creature of Man, and we have something more repellent than Atheism. But let us look, further, at its consequences. We are told that the Infinite Spirit shall awake when the last of the series comes; but it is necessary to this theory that the last should never come. If humanity were capable of coming to an end, then the Infinite Spirit would after all have a limited dwelling-place, just as truly as if He inhabited a single individual form. If, therefore, the Left admit the possibility of a last man, they virtually abandon their own position, which is the impossibility of the Infinite having its manifestation in the finite. We repeat, then, that this theory requires an endless existence of the human race; but if so, what follows? This, for one thing, that God can never become Personal, can never recognise Himself, can never awake into the consciousness of His own being. And then the question suggests itself, Why believe in such a God at all? or if we do believe in Him, why call Him by a divine name, seeing He has no divine attributes, not even consciousness? This is a question which many of the Left have been candid enough to answer. Feurbach was not long in perceiving that his God was a vanishing quantity; he therefore dismissed Him from his system, and proclaimed religion to be the worship of humanity. But the Left could not stop even here; how could even humanity be to them an object of worship when that humanity can never be completed, can never find its head or culmination? The Left found that they would need to go farther, and they did it; they dismissed religion altogether. The question which Strauss asks in his latest work, 'Have we any longer a religion?' and which he answers, upon the whole, in the negative, is only the legitimate conclusion drawn from the premises of his predecessors; and at this point the spiritualism of Germany meets hand in hand with the positivism of France. In one sense, the Left, in its latest development, has surpassed the philosophy of Comte. Comte was a positivist; but he had sense enough to perceive that religious feelings were themselves positive impressions, and therefore he constructed a religion of his own. But to the Left, religious feelings are not realities, but illusions; they are the product of the individual mind, and in the system of the Left the individual mind is nothing; the race, and the race alone, exists. Bruno Bauer denounces what he calls pectoral theology, by which he means simply the sentiments of the heart. According to him, no individual man has any right to assume that he is a recipient of divine impressions, or to accord to his religious convictions any higher place than that of human imaginings of things unknown and unknowable. The philosophers of the Left, therefore, have outstripped the legitimate boundaries even of positivism. Positivism proclaims that the individual mind has not arrived at any experience beyond that of temporal phenomena; the Left Hegelianism goes a step farther still, and proclaims that the individual mind cannot, without contradicting

The Right and the Left. 125

its own nature, ever, through all the ages, arrive at the knowledge of God.

We have now set before the student the distinctive principles of the Right and the Left. We have endeavoured to show that the former is consistent with the essential features of the Reformed and Lutheran Theology, and that the latter, if pressed out to its logical consequences, is identical with Atheism itself. We believe that between these extremes there is no intermediate course. It is well known that attempts have been made in certain quarters to steer a middle way, avoiding the difficulties of either side, and adopting the advantages of each. It is our decided conviction that these attempts have signally failed, and therefore we shall not interrupt the subject to offer any explanation of them. We shall, however, append to the close of this chapter a note, in which we shall endeavour to enumerate what seems to us to be the principal efforts at reconciliation which have been attempted between the two Hegelian schools. We do not consider the study of this point one of much importance; we are convinced that a middle view is untenable; and therefore, while we shall mention the schools of reconciliation, we do not think that the student's knowledge of German theology will be materially injured by passing them over. In the meantime, let us just inquire for a moment into the soundness of that foundation on which the system of the Left reposes. It all rests upon one principle, and that is, the impossibility that an Infinite Being should be manifested in a finite form. If this principle be true, the system must be allowed to be impregnable; if it be false, the whole structure must fall to the ground. Now it may be conceded that every theory which has succeeded in obtaining a large number of adherents must have within it a certain measure of truth; a doctrine which was absolutely false could not exist for an hour. The fact, therefore, that the Left has secured so many votaries is a proof that at least it must have one side of the truth. The first point to determine is the meaning of the word infinite. There are clearly two distinct senses in which this term is employed. We sometimes apply it to the body, at others to the soul. Now the infinitude of a body and the infinitude of a soul are not only different, but in some respects even contrary things. An infinite body would be a body boundless in extent—that is to say, a gigantic mass of matter, filling every corner of all possible space. An infinite soul would be a spiritual intelligence possessed of all possible perfections, but having no necessary relation to space at all. An infinite world must occupy the whole field of immensity. An infinite soul is no bigger than a mathematical point—in other words, it has no magnitude at all; we measure its infinitude not by its extent, but by its intensity. An infinite straight line is a straight line without end; infinite love is love without a flaw. It will readily appear, then, that when the Left assure us that the infinite cannot be manifested in a finite form, we must first ask them what they mean by the infinite? Do they believe God to be a gigantic piece of matter, unlimited in extent? If so, then they are right; an infinite body cannot exist within a finite body, any more than a large house can be enclosed within the walls of a cottage. But the question recurs, Is this the natural conception of God? is it not more reasonable to regard God as a Spirit than to view Him as a material organism? And if we take our stand on the spirituality of God, we shall find the case altogether changed. Is there any contradiction in supposing that infinite love could inhabit the form of a human being? Love fills no space, occupies no room. There is no more contradiction in a human form being inhabited by a love which is infinite, than there is in the same form being inhabited by a love which is finite, for in the spiritual world the infinite is no larger than the finite; it is distinguished from it not by its size, but by its intensity, its warmth, its fervour. It is a favourite dictum of the Left, that no idea can be perfectly manifested by one individual mind. In one sense the saying is true; in another it is false. There are two ways in which an idea may be manifested,—in its extent and prevalence, or in its force and clearness. Let us say, for example, that the national idea of Great Britain is that of bravery; this idea might be revealed either extensively or intensively. It would be revealed extensively if every man, woman, and child in the United Kingdom were patterns of valour. Of course an individual could not do this; it would be a contradiction in terms. But the national idea of Great Britain could be revealed by a single individual in another way,—by an intense exhibition of bravery in his own person. What do we mean by the phrase *representative men*? Do we not intend to convey that every nation has certain individuals who exhibit its characteristics in such perfection that they may be taken to represent the nation itself? By the very use of this phrase do we not deny the position of the Left? Now the Christian conception of God is that of love; love, according to Christianity, is the idea which sums up the universe. Is there any contradiction in the assertion that some eighteen centuries ago this idea of infinite love found its perfect illustration and embodiment in a finite form and a human soul? There is certainly nothing in philosophy which is at variance with such a thought. It never can be said with truth that a material finitude can exclude a spiritual infinitude. During the Middle Ages there was a serious discussion among the Schoolmen, which has become to us in modern times a favourite subject of ridicule. The point debated was, How many angels could dance on the point of a needle? It is all very well to laugh, but it is really the question between the Right and the Left in Germany, and must be answered in precisely the same way. For is it not manifest that the whole discussion of the Schoolmen hinges upon one point: Is an angel material, or purely spiritual? If angels be conceived as purely spiritual intelligences, there would certainly be no absurdity in supposing that all the celestial beings in the universe could at one and the same moment be concentrated even in so small a space as the Schoolmen indicated; for while we must think of spiritual intelligences as inhabiting space, we cannot conceive of them as occupying any room in it. The question, therefore, which has been started by the Left, as to the possibility of the Infinite co-existing with the finite, is nothing more nor less than a revival of that old medieval dispute, at which we are accustomed to look back with self-complacent raillery. The fact is suggestive and instructive. It may serve to remind us that the difficulties we encounter in our religious speculations are not the result of superior genius or increased enlightenment, but are merely the reproduction in new forms of struggles long past, and problems of other minds. It may tend to impress us afresh with that changeless truth, the unity of Man in every age, and may lead us to see the limitations of thought which environ us only as the repetition and resurrection of long buried conflicts, which in the days of old perplexed our brother men.

It may seem strange that the theology of the Left, founded as it is upon a manifest misconception, should yet have attained in Germany to such a wide-spread influence; for it cannot be denied that this side of the Hegelian philosophy, which we believe to be the erroneous one, has nevertheless succeeded in obtaining the mastery over its more orthodox opponent, and has resulted in plunging Germany into an abyss of Materialism. Perhaps, however, it is only natural that the more heterodox side of the system should for the time have prevailed. It seems to us like the instinct of the child who has received a new and curious toy to break it open, in order to discover what is in the inside of it. The Hegelian system came to Germany as a new thing; it was like a wonderful piece of mechanism which could be applied to an infinite number of uses —which could be made equally powerful either for destruction or reconstruction. The mind of Germany was naturally eager to analyse this wonderful instrument, to cut it up into its component parts, and see what each of these parts if taken separately would lead to. It has done so, and has found what the child finds in the broken toy—nothing. Here is the goal to which all the speculations of the Left have inevitably led,—the absolute negation of all knowledge, the eternal gulf which intervenes between the individual soul and the unknown Infinite Spirit. That Spirit itself is neither a person nor a life, but an empty abstraction, a name for that mysterious limit which bounds the horizon of Man; and Feurbach has only expressed the necessary and final resort of the system when he has declared the sum of his religion to be this: 'We adore the great negation.' Yet, dark as is the picture, may we not gather hope from its very darkness? It is the doctrine of Hegel himself that in every stage of life, and in every department of study, the blackest night must precede the day, that death must be the forerunner of life, that suffering is the necessary precursor of joy. May we not expect,

The Right and the Left.

from the very law of that system which the Left professes to follow; that the intensity of its midnight will prove the harbinger of its morning, and that from the depth of those ruins which indicate the progress of its destructive hand there shall rise a brighter and a purer temple, where men shall worship in spirit and in truth?

NOTE.—As representatives of the Left, we may take Bruno Bauer, F. C. Baur of Tübingen, Feurbach, Hitzig, Michelet, Nobel, Strauss, Vatche, and originally Schelling. To the Right belong Hegel himself, Daub, Marheinecke, Schaller, Erdmann, and Schelling in his second stage. The following are the principal attempts which have been made to reconcile the extremes:—

1st. There is a class of theologians, called sometimes Post-Hegelians, at others Pseudo-Hegelians, represented by the younger Fichte, Fischer, Weisse, Branez, and Schelling in his last period. They hold that there is something in Deity behind either the soul or the body, viz. the fact of existence itself: the soul and body are only the manifestations of this existence, and the Being or the Ego lies behind its manifestations. This is no reconciliation, but rather a departure from the Hegelian philosophy. Hegel denies that there can be any conscious existence which is not awakened by external contact.

2d. Another party, represented chiefly by Rosencranz, attempts to reconcile the Right and Left by holding that, while the life of the individual cannot manifest the divine life, it may yet serve to illustrate it. This we take to be a contradiction in terms; every illustration of a truth is to some extent a manifestation of it.

3*d*. The only plausible attempt to mediate between the parties is that which has been made by the party which might be termed Evangelical Hegelians, being divided between Hegel and Schleiermacher. Its leaders are Goschel, Dorner, Martensen, Liebner, Rothe, and Lange. They concede to the Left that the Infinite cannot be manifested in a single individual, because an individual only comes to know himself in contrast to others, and therefore limitation is necessary to his being. But these theologians say, this does not prove that God is not Personal; it rather proves that the individual is not personal. Individuality requires limitation; personality excludes limitation. God therefore is, strictly speaking, the only Person. The Son of man is not a separate individual; He is the union of all individuals—He is the head of an organism or body of which each individual man is only one of the members. Accordingly in Him the Infinite can fully dwell, because He is not a unit, but a unity, a collective life which embraces within itself all other lives, an ocean of which we are but the drops. On this view we can only repeat a remark which we have already made. If the Son of man sums up in Himself all the individuals of humanity, He is Himself an individual after all, for individuality is nothing more nor less than completedness; whatever cannot be summed up is infinite, whatever can is finite or individual. In spite, therefore, of their attempt at mediation, Goschel and his followers are really adherents of the Right Hegelianism.

CHAPTER XII.

MYTHICAL THEORY OF STRAUSS.[1]

IT will readily appear that the predominance obtained by the Left over German thought must have exercised an inevitable influence on the principles of biblical interpretation. It is the distinctive doctrine of the Left that the individual is nothing, and that individual modes of thinking are worthy of no attention. The necessary result of this opinion is a contempt for historical records: history, being a mere finite manifestation, in other words a collection of individual sentiments, must be regarded as destitute of all authority, and as deriving all its importance from the inward truth which it symbolizes. Nor was it long before this tendency of the Left made itself apparent in a very formidable shape. Not more than three years after the death of Hegel, and in that immediately following the demise of Schleiermacher, there appeared upon the scene a man of transcendent critical talents, deeply read in the systems of his predecessors

[1] The student will observe that we have not, in considering the mythical theory, taken account of Strauss' latest work, *The Old Faith and the New;* we have referred this to another stage of development.

and contemporaries, and prepared to investigate the truth without any theological bias. That man was David Strauss. In 1835 he was but seven-and-twenty; yet in that year he rose at once to his meridian, and obtained instantaneously an influence over his country which others had taken long to win. His was one of those natures in which mind predominates over soul. Standing at the opposite remove from Schleiermacher, he considered the testimony of feeling to be of no value, and looked upon individual impressions as destitute of any authority. In his own person, so far as his character can be learned from his writings, he had succeeded in crucifying the emotional part of his nature, if indeed he ever possessed it. He was calm, unimpassioned, cold-blooded, thoroughly phlegmatic. He betrayed no personal animosity, and seldom indulged in any personality; he attacked theories, but not men. His writings are cold and clear, unusually clear for a German. He indulges in no circumlocution, but goes right to the point, and at once reveals his aim. He speaks without impulse and without vehemence. Now and then, indeed, there is heard a muttered sound of underground humour, but it is not prolonged, and interrupts not the strokes of the hammer of destruction; for Strauss is essentially a destroyer of all historical truth. He professes, as we have said, to have no theological bias, but he has a very decided anti-theological one; he assumes the impossibility of miraculous interpositions. It will be found universally, that those who cry out most loudly against writing a book with a dogmatic bias in favour of theological truth, have themselves conceived a pretty strong prejudice against the acceptance of that truth on any evidence. The mind is not a sheet of white paper, though Locke says it is; we are never unbiased; he that is not for the truth is against it. It is in vain, therefore, for the critic to pretend that he, any more than other men, is beyond the influence of presupposition. If he is not influenced by a prepossession in favour of religion, he is actuated by a motive impelling him in the contrary direction, and the one as much as the other belongs to the domain of dogma. Strauss comes to his work with a dogma in his mind, which he desires to see verified by the testimony of experience. That dogma is the impossibility of miraculous interference, or, to put it into the language of the Left, the impossibility that the Infinite Spirit can find a manifestation in the lives of finite individuals. But let us proceed briefly to examine his own theory.

The system of Strauss has an external and an internal side. Its external aspect is this: Throughout the Old Testament history we find a gradual accumulation of Jewish legends around an imaginary personage, to whose coming the people looked forward with the eager expectancy of those who wait for the realization of their dreams. Whatever great acts in their history were said to be performed by any of their leaders must be repeated by their Messiah in exaggerated form. Accordingly, when there appeared one whose character and bearing rendered him conspicuous amongst his countrymen, they simply allowed these legends to cluster round him, until in the course of time they became indelibly associated with his name, and his original earthly life was lost and obliterated in that ideal existence with which imagination had invested him. This is the external side of the system of Strauss; but it has also an internal aspect. He regards the idea of the Messiah as itself mythical—that is to say, as the personification of an abstract truth. According to Strauss, the Messianic idea is nothing more nor less than the description of humanity itself, the picturing of the human race as if it were a single man. Humanity is the child of invisible parents, Spirit being its father and Nature its mother. As it is produced by Nature out of the ordinary course of things, it may be said poetically to be born of a virgin. It does not at once after birth come into full consciousness of its power and glory; for the field of life which it enters has already been occupied by that very Nature which has given it birth, and the mother is at variance with her child: it comes unto its own, and its own receives it not. Nature would fain drag it down to her own level, but humanity will not be so denuded of its birthright; it has a father as well as a mother, and that father is the Infinite Spirit. The result is a violent struggle between life and death, a struggle in which for the time humanity seems to be vanquished; it is crucified, and the life of Nature triumphs over it. By and by, however, from the very depth of its ruin there comes hope, and death becomes the progenitor of life. Humanity bursts the bonds of Nature, and rises from the grave of its corruption into resurrection glory, being received up, as it were, into its native heaven, and the cross is transfigured into the crown.

The student will here carefully observe the sense in which Strauss employs the word mythical. With him it does not mean fabulous, but simply spiritual, as opposed to historical. He admits that the statements of the gospel are true; he only denies that they are historically true. Strange as it may seem, it did not occur to Strauss that by such a theory he put himself beyond the pale of the Church. It did not appear to him that by the profession of such views he was called upon in honour to resign his office as a Christian minister. On the contrary, he endeavours to reduce to a minimum the difference between the historical believer and the mythical believer. His reasoning amounts to this: An evangelical preacher selects, perhaps, for the subject of his discourse the narrative of Christ walking on the sea. He begins by a reference to the outward circumstances of the case, by a description of the scene, and an enumeration of the external incidents. Yet upon these even the evangelical preacher does not long linger. He speedily passes on to derive suggestions from the outward picture, to spiritualize the narrative into practical lessons for everyday life, to show that there is always an Infinite Presence even amidst the sea of human trouble, and how, by surrendering our souls to that Presence,

Mythical Theory of Strauss. 139

there is always heard the still small voice, 'Peace, be still.' The mythical preacher proclaims the same gospel, with this one difference, that what the evangelical minister calls the practical lessons derived from the subject, the mythical preacher calls the subject itself. To him the spiritual inferences of the passage are the primary truths. These truths are not derived from the history, it is the history that is derived from them; the outward incident is only a poetical representation of eternal truth. And so the mythical preacher simply passes over that historical reference, on which even his evangelical brother dwells so lightly, and without adverting at all to the outward circumstances of his text, he proceeds at once to unfold its spiritual import.

Such is the defence which Strauss offers of his desire to retain the office of the Christian ministry. We have mentioned it merely with the view of pointing out to the student the sense in which he employs the word mythical—that is, as a designation of spiritual as opposed to historical truth. Now there is one thing which on the very threshold of this theory strikes us with peculiar interest, and it is this, that with all his destructiveness Strauss makes an important concession to Christianity; he acknowledges it to be spiritually true. In this respect the scepticism of our day is much less dangerous and much nearer to a return than the scepticism of last century. Deplorable as, to every earnest mind, must ever be these attempts to remove those landmarks of antiquity which have been consecrated by so many hallowed memories, deeply as the philosophy of the Left has been implicated in these efforts to obliterate the historical past, there is yet in this last phase of negative criticism some glimmering of a returning sun, in the prominence given to that spiritual basis of truth which underlies the gospel narrative. The Deists of the preceding century occupied a far inferior platform; they opposed Christianity because they held it to be contrary to reason. To Strauss and the school of Strauss, Christianity is the very essence of human reason; and if these theologians of the Left reject it, it is not because they think it in antagonism with human life, but rather because they believe it to be itself so life-like that its existence might be imagined even where it had no reality. And that is the reason why so many valuable works on Christian evidences have in our century been consigned to comparative oblivion. It is no uncommon thing to hear surprise expressed that such a book as Butler's *Analogy*, attracting as it did the merited attention and admiration of the men of its own day, should with us have fallen into an almost total neglect, and be remembered chiefly as a relic of the past. But the surprise will be moderated if we reflect for a moment that the grounds of the controversy have altogether altered. The field of battle is no longer the same, the weapons of warfare are entirely different, the very opponents of Christianity are another race of beings. Butler wrote his *Analogy* to a generation which held the essence of the Christian religion to be antagonistic to human reason; and in opposition to that generation, he endeavoured to show that the facts of the gospel have their ground in the life of Man. But Strauss and the sceptics of our day admit the whole substance of Butler's *Analogy ;* if Butler had been living, they would have hailed him as an ally. They hold as strongly as ever he did that the facts recorded in the gospel have their ground in human nature, but they make this very truth an evidence against historical Christianity. They say that human nature, finding these principles within herself, cast them out of herself into an assemblage of outward forms and images, very valuable as vivid illustrations, but destitute of all historical authority. They tell us that historical Christianity is nothing more nor less than the poetical garniture in which, during a period of high imaginative force, the idea of humanity has clothed itself. They would ask Butler why it is that the outward facts of the gospel find so many points of contact with the inward intuitions of the soul, and they would tell him that the reason of their analogy is the simple truth that the history of the Bible is only the personification of the thoughts of Man. We repeat that, one-sided and untenable as such a position must ever be, it makes at least one grand concession to the truth of the gospel narrative when it declares the narrative to be spiritually true. In so doing it takes a higher ground than that scepticism which has passed away,—the scepticism of Bolingbroke, of Chubb, of Collins, of the French Illuminati, which finds in the facts of Christianity a barrier to human reason, and rejects the testimony of Scripture as a contradiction to the life of the soul.

Nevertheless, this position of Strauss is one which is beset with difficulties, at the least as great as those which he professes to discover in historical Christianity. An examination of these difficulties belongs rather to the sphere of apologetics than of theological exposition; yet even here there are one or two points which may be briefly glanced at. Strauss has entered into an elaborate review of the contradictions and seeming impossibilities which beset an acceptance of the gospel narrative. Has he well considered and carefully pondered those many hindrances to acceptance by which his own system is encompassed? Is he prepared to show how a nation, whose leading thought was the infinite separation between God and Man, should yet have adopted as its central truth the Incarnation of the divine in the human? Is he prepared to point out that law of the human mind by which a people essentially empirical and sensuous in their mode of thinking should yet have been able to formulate a system of abstract philosophy, of which modern Germany is only the echo and the pattern? Is he prepared to explain why the Jews, who looked for a miracle-working Messiah, should yet have been content to accept as the fulfilment of their hopes one who during his life did not work miracles, but who only received the reputation of it after he had passed away? Is he in a position to enlighten us how it came to pass that a nation whose Messianic ideal was that of a conqueror, of a temporal deliverer, of a warrior king, should yet have attached itself to one whose professed and leading aim was perfection through suffering and redemption through death? We know very well that even in the Old Testament there are pictures of a suffering Messiah; but we know also that long before the birth of Jesus these pictures had been totally obliterated, and those of the conqueror alone remained. Is he able to defend his own theory by showing how a mythical representation of Jesus could arise within thirty years of His actual life on earth? For it is a notorious fact, that if at this moment the four recognised Gospels could be proved to be forgeries, there would still remain a fifth Gospel, whose authenticity even Strauss does not deny, which assumes all the leading facts of the four, and which is admittedly little more than five-and-twenty years older than the death of Jesus; we mean the Epistles of Paul to the Galatians, Corinthians, and Romans.[1] Above all, even putting these difficulties aside, is Strauss prepared to account for the fact, which even he must admit to be a fact, that all history has found its centre in a single Man? Why should the spirit of mythology have enshrined itself in Jesus rather than in any other being of that age or of previous ages? Is the Christ of Strauss such a being as to justify his countrymen in surrounding his head with a wreath of mythical glory? In his first *Life of Jesus*, he tells us repeatedly what an impression Christ must have made by the greatness of his personal

[1] See supplementary note, page 210.

character; but nowhere in this work does he inform us wherein that greatness consisted. He himself appears conscious that in this respect his book has been defective, that it has not even fulfilled the promise of its title-page. Accordingly he has produced another *Life of Jesus*, written in a popular style, and intended not for scholars, but for the German people, and here he has sought to supply the omission so fatal to his first undertaking. Here at length, with some degree of prominence, we are introduced to the personal Christ according to the gospel of Strauss, and have an opportunity of judging for ourselves how far such a Christ could have revolutionized the world. There is brought before us a young man in whose person were united two opposite tendencies, the one Jewish, the other Hellenic. The Jewish tendency is the result of his birth, and seeks to bind him to the institutions and ceremonies of his country; the Hellenic is the result of his disposition, and impresses him with a sense of nearness to God, which impels him to break through the ceremonial limitations of his race, to dispense with the mediation of priest and sacrifice, and to realize his immediate union with the Infinite I Am. We ask if there is anything in such a character which would render Christ worthy of divine honour from His countrymen. We ask if there is anything in such a conception which would even mark Him out from the rest of mankind. Is it so peculiar a thing to have a struggle of tendencies in our nature? is there any man altogether without such a struggle? Is it so peculiar a thing in history to find one conscious of his immediate union with the Father of Spirits? Are not the mystics of the Middle Ages a refutation of such a doctrine? Is it so peculiar a thing to find even a Jewish mind struggling to break away from the narrowness of its own nationality, and actually succeeding in surmounting the limits of its race and lineage? So far is it from being so, that Philo and all the Alexandrian Jews in general may be quoted as examples of the same experience. The Christ of Strauss, then, does not explain Christianity, does not even account for the estimate formed of his own greatness. So far from being an object of attraction, he is barely an object of interest to the mind, and fails to explain that revolution which has been kindled by the mention of his name. Christianity, whatever it may have been at first, is now at least a living historical fact—has been a living historical fact for the last eighteen hundred years. That fact stands waiting for explanation, and any theory which does not explain it is not entitled to credence. The theory of Strauss, by the admission even of negative criticism, has not succeeded in its aim; and the succession of attempts, equally wild and equally abortive, which have been made to supply its defects, is alone a proof and a monument of its inadequacy and its failure.

CHAPTER XIII.

BREAKING UP OF THE MYTHICAL THEORY—SCHOOL OF TÜBINGEN.

THE mythical theory narrowly escaped strangulation almost at the hour of its birth, and that not from the defenders of historical Christianity, but from the retainers of its own household. Nearly synchronical with the publication of Strauss' *Life of Jesus*, Bruno Bauer appeared upon the stage with another theory, which, if it had obtained acceptance, would have effectually and for ever suppressed the foregoing speculations. The view of Bruno Bauer was not, any more than that of Strauss, intended to be friendly to Christianity; but it was of such a nature that both theories could not be true, and that the adoption of the one must destroy the other. Strauss, it will be remembered, regarded the gospel history as an accumulation of Old Testament legends around an imaginary person, to whose coming as king and deliverer men had been looking forward for ages. But Bruno Bauer rejects such a notion as untenable, stigmatizes the legends as meaningless, and denies that previous to the birth of Jesus there ever had been any general expectation of a

Messiah. He regards the Messianic idea as the immediate creation of the Church, and the Church itself he regards as a reaction of Jewish liberty against the oppression of the Roman Empire; but according to him, neither the Church nor the Messianic idea had any definite existence before the Christian era. Christianity thus ceases to be a development, and is viewed as a sudden ebullition, which had its ground partly in the awakening of self-consciousness into freedom, but still more in the deliberate creation of a new idea, that of the historical Messiah.

Now, had matters ended here, the mythical theory would have suffered little. In point of ability, in grasp of its subject, and in depth of scientific research, the work of Bruno Bauer was far inferior to that of Strauss, and its influence over German thought has been limited in the extreme. But the mission of this work was not so much to found a school as to inaugurate an era; its chief design was to break ground in opposition to the mythical theory, and to leave the completion of the process to be wrought out by abler hands. Its doctrine of a suddenly-created Messianic belief was so manifestly contrary to fact, that no amount of talent or learning could ever have obtained it credence; and as that doctrine was not supported by any great exhibition either of talent or of learning, the work of Bruno Bauer would have speedily been consigned to oblivion, if its attack upon the mythical theory had not been followed up by a far more distinguished and a far more dangerous adversary. In

1838 there stood forth in the front ranks of German theology one of the greatest biblical critics, and one of the profoundest speculative minds which this or perhaps any age has ever seen; we mean Professor Baur of Tübingen. He was deeply imbued with the Hegelian philosophy, and was resolved to push that method of inquiry to its uttermost limits. He had attached himself to the party of the Left, and was therefore, like Strauss, an enemy to historical Christianity; yet he was not prepared to adopt that explanation by which Strauss had endeavoured to account for its existence. He proposed an altogether different scheme,—a scheme which, if accepted, would prove equally adverse alike to historical truth and to her mythical antagonist. The leading features of his system are briefly these. We are apt to think of the portraiture of Christ in the New Testament as one united whole, but in reality it is not so. The truth is, that the New Testament exhibits three distinct pictures of Christ. In the first of these He is described after a Jewish type—that is, as a man who, in reward for his rectitude, has been gifted by God with the possession of supernatural power. In the second He is represented after the Gentile conception; and here He wears an aspect higher than that of Judaism. We find throughout Gentile religions the idea very prevalent that the gods were incarnate in human form, and hence, according to this conception Christ is represented as an emanation of the divine. The third picture is that which reconciles the other two; Christ after the Jewish manner receives supernatural gifts, but it is only as a sign or outward manifestation of His own inward greatness. The first of these is the view of Matthew, James, Peter, and Jude; the second of Luke and the Pauline Epistles; and the third of the Gospel of John.

Such are the facts as they appear in the system of Baur. His next object is to account for these facts, and he does so in the following manner:—The three different pictures of Christ are the result of three different tendencies. Judaism tended to separate God and Man in such a manner that everything which the divine communicated to the human must be in the form of a gift. Heathenism, on the other hand, leant towards the union of God and Man, and therefore everything which God communicated must be a part of Himself. There was a third party, which could not exclusively be classed under either of these, but which in some measure shared the nature of both. It consisted of those Jews of Alexandria who, after the conquest of their country by Alexander, had chosen to forget the land of their fathers, and had sought as much as possible to amalgamate their manners and religion with the religion and manners of the surrounding Gentile nations. Hence the peculiarity of this party was its eclecticism, its desire to find truth in everything. Its distinguishing prerogative was to reconcile differences, and all its works were of a reconciliatory nature. From it proceeded the fourth Gospel, whose design was to draw the portraiture of a Christ who would neither exhibit the merely supernatural gifts bestowed upon a righteous man, as the Jewish Christians held, nor yet the mere emanations of a divine Being entirely separate from humanity, as the Gentiles were prone to hold, but who would reveal the aspect of one at once perfectly divine and perfectly human—divine from the perfection of His humanity, and perfectly human because He was divine.

Now in one view this theory of Baur is, if possible, more unfavourable to historical Christianity than even that of Strauss. With all his mythicism, Strauss had at least allowed a certain amount of interest to centre around the actual person of Christ. But here, for all the place it occupies in the system, the person of Christ might be obliterated altogether. Who Christ really was Baur never inquires; what we are told of Him he regards as merely a series of ideal portraits, intended to give currency to the views of different parties then existing in the Church. His sentiments concerning the actual Christ are not badly expressed by Schwegler, one of his own school, when he says, 'We know not who He was.' None of the portraits contained in the four Gospels is older, according to Baur, than the year 130 A.D.; all the intervening space between this date and the opening of the Christian era is regarded as a blank in sacred history, which is not bridged over by any reliable monuments of antiquity, nor illuminated by any trustworthy records. A more dreary prospect to the historical student than that which this theory unfolds cannot well be conceived. The origin of Christianity, the person of its Founder, the circumstances which ushered it into the world, the struggles and conflicts which opposed its progress, the influences which accelerated its growth, the names and lives of its earliest votaries, and the actual facts which gave rise to the Gospel narratives, are all consigned to the sphere of entire conjecture, and left in a region of obscurity into whose depths no light of research or investigation has yet been able to penetrate. Indeed, in contemplating this picture, one is prone to apply to himself the words addressed of old to the Samaritan, and to say of the believers in Christianity, 'They worship they know not what.' If the theory of Baur be true, our belief is centred not in something which happened at the opening of the Christian era, but in something which occurred towards the middle of the second century; we see the stream, indeed, but we have lost the fountain-head; we have a vision of the vast ocean, but we are no longer able to trace the course of those rivers which have swelled it. In this respect, therefore, the theory of Baur is more unhistorical than that of its predecessor, more mythical in its design and aim, more adverse to those outward landmarks which reveal the footprints of truth.

But while in one aspect it undoubtedly is so, while there is a sense in which the theory of Baur is, in the depth of its mythicism, even in advance of that of Strauss, there is another and a more important sense, in which it is altogether a revolt from the mythical theory. It will be observed that, according to Baur and the Tübingen school, the portraits of Christ contained in our Gospels were created for the purpose of supporting different tendencies of thought. Now that which is created for a purpose is no longer mythical. Nothing can be mythical which does not grow up unconsciously. We do not call the work of the poet a myth, for we know it to be the result of deliberate forethought, the product of many anxious hours, the external manifestation of a long-contemplated ideal. And so, if we suppose with Baur that the lives of Christ which we possess were the result of artistic creation, and designed to supply a special want of the age in which they were written, we are not at liberty any longer to hold with Strauss that these lives were mythical, the unconscious and spontaneous imaginings by which the human mind sought to give its hopes reality. We cannot at one and the same moment believe both theories. We may say with Baur that Christianity was created by the conflict of different schools, or with Strauss that it came forth undesignedly from the depth of the human consciousness, but we cannot accept both views; if one be true, the other must be false. It is thus that in every age the opposition to historical Christianity has presented itself not in a uniform aspect, but as a house divided against itself; and those who in their attack upon the Christian citadel form one united army, are ready immediately after the battle to engage in conflict amongst themselves. Even the grosser form of Rationalism was not able to preserve an intrinsic uniformity. What can be more different than the standpoints of Wegscheider and Paulus? Equally opposed as they are to the admission of a miraculous element, their interpretation of Scripture is contrary in the extreme,—the former treating its statements as symbolical accommodations to human thought, the latter accepting them as the literal narration of mere natural occurrences. Or if we pass from the grosser Rationalism in its own inherent inconsistencies to the direct opposition which it encounters in the mythical theory, we find another powerful illustration of the house divided against itself. Ernest Renan the Frenchman and David Strauss the German are at one in their opposition to Christianity, but diametrically opposed to each other as to where its weak point lies. And now we find that not even the mythical theory itself has been able to escape being rent asunder by its professed friends; for we have seen that the school of Tübingen, which in one sense has grown out of the mythicism of Strauss, presents to that mythicism on another side a barrier so formidable, that the one theory can only exist by the sacrifice of the other. It is in vain that Strauss in his later *Life of Jesus* seeks to amalgamate his views with those of Baur. It is in vain he endeavours to supplement his theory of the Scripture history by incorporating with it Baur's account of the Scripture origin. Artlessness cannot lie side by side with deliberate design, nor can spontaneous mythology be found harmoniously united to a carefully matured imposture. The things are contrary one to the other, and must ever remain in mutual antagonism. The theory of Baur refuses to coalesce with that of its predecessor, and therefore the success of the one in its assault upon historical truth would inevitably involve the discomfiture of the other.

And what shall we say of the theory of Baur itself? It will be remembered that in speaking of Strauss we found that, amidst all his destructiveness, he had at least made one great concession to the truth of Christianity, by finding a basis for it in the depth of the human consciousness. And so we think it will be found that Baur, amidst the many dark features of his system, has yet unwittingly to himself made an admission which, if carried out to its legitimate result, would go far to reconstruct what he has destroyed. Baur says that the tendencies of Jew and Gentile, which, according to him, account for the whole of Christianity, were ultimately reconciled and united. Now let us see what this amounts to. When two things can be reconciled, it proves that there is something common to both of them, and deeper than either of them; if it were not so, their union would be impossible. If the Jewish and Gentile tendencies admit of reconciliation, it can only be because these tendencies themselves are subordinate to something else, something greater than both, which can exist in spite of both and finally reunite both. And we may be very sure that the thing to be accounted for is not the tendencies, but just that connecting object between them which neither of them separately can destroy, and which has power eventually to obliterate both together in a common unity. We may be very sure that, whatever this connecting link may be, it will be found to be nothing less than the essence of Christianity itself. What, then, is this mysterious bond, which runs through all differences of opinion, and forms a meeting-ground for the most diverse schools of thought? What is it but the Person of the Redeemer Himself? In Him all tendencies meet; in Him the religions of the world, ready to vanish away, find a new life and a new significance. In Christ, the centre of history, the tendencies of Jew and Gentile are originally combined. In Him for the first time these vastly-contrasted phases of thought are found existing side by side. The removal of His outward presence destroys for a while their unity, and makes them discordant again; but the influence of that presence is stronger than the influence of school, or sect, or party, and by the power of that common brotherhood which the life of the Master has diffused through humanity, the temporary wall of partition which His absence has created gradually moulders away, and allows a free expanse to the sunshine of universal love. This we believe to be the only philosophical, as it is the only scriptural, explanation of the meeting of the nations around Christianity. So far from that concurrence being the cause of the gospel, it requires itself the gospel to account for it, and finds its solution in that great truth which is at once the centre of history and the foundation of spiritual religion,—the union of the Infinite with the finite.

CHAPTER XIV.

BREAKING UP OF THE MYTHICAL THEORY CONTINUED—SIGNS OF A RETURN TO THE OLD RATIONALISM.

IT was not long before the mythical theory was assailed from another and a very different direction. We have seen that Rationalism had been destroyed by Kant, and in one sense it had been effectually destroyed; it never could reappear in precisely the same form. Mythicism came in its room, and the standpoint of these two was a contrary one. Rationalism had accepted the facts of Scripture, but had offered a natural explanation of them; Mythicism denied the existence of the facts, and regarded them as mere symbols of spiritual truth. Both systems were extreme views, and extremes, by their very nature, cannot stand. Accordingly we have seen Mythicism, like Rationalism, ready to vanish away, and prepared to leave the field to some other competitor. We have said that that field could never again be occupied by Rationalism in its original form; but this did not prevent its resurrection in a new form. When an old system rises from the dead, it must rise with a modified aspect. It finds the world permeated by an altogether different atmosphere to that in which at first it had its being; and it is inevitable that the new atmosphere should exert a corresponding influence upon the old system. Accordingly, when Rationalism came forth from that grave in which Kant had laid her, she unconsciously appropriated the fruits of that progress which the world had since achieved, and improved the natural roughness of her form by selecting her apparel from the fairest robes of the systems which surrounded her.

This modern revival of the old Rationalism has found two conspicuous representatives, the one in France, the other in Germany: we mean, of course, Renan and Schenkel. Not that these representatives of Rationalism travel by the same road; they are as different in the form of their statement as their respective nations differ in the form of their thought. Renan is a Frenchman, and his Christ is a Parisian; Schenkel is a German, and his Christ is of Teutonic race. The Christ of Renan is conceived after the French ideal,— a fair Galilean growing up amidst beautiful scenery, and experiencing within himself a consciousness of God, which he longs to realize in a divine kingdom upon earth. The Christ of Schenkel is also conceived after a national type, but it is German, not French; this Christ is a heretic, a broad churchman, contending with the hierarchy or orthodox men of that day, and seeking to secure for his countrymen the liberty of religious thought. The Christ of Renan does not at first claim to be the Messiah, but advances that claim only afterwards, and employs imposture to support it. Strange to say, it does not strike Renan that the hero of his romance is made less beautiful by this subterfuge. He tells us gravely that every idea must stoop in order to realize itself, forgetting that there is a difference between the stooping of self-abnegation and the stooping of selfish meanness. The German is here far ahead of the Frenchman. The Christ of Schenkel, like the Christ of Renan, comes to the idea of his Messiahship at a later period of his life; but with Schenkel it is not an imposture, but a development. The Christ of Renan pretends to work miracles; the Christ of Schenkel works no miracles, nor does he pretend to do so; he merely performs certain acts, which astonish his contemporaries, and which are magnified by the succeeding age into prodigies of miraculous power. This view of Schenkel comes as near as possible to a revival of the Rationalism of Paulus. No doubt both with him and Renan there is a certain adhesion of the mythical element. Neither the Christ of Schenkel nor the Christ of Renan is the Messiah of the gospel. They construct an ideal out of their own brain, shape it according to the pattern of modern feelings and customs, and throw back upon the soil of Judea the thoughts which belong only to their own century in general, and which pertain in particular to the atmosphere of Paris and Berlin. None would object more vehemently than they to the adoption of such a course by the orthodox defenders of Christianity. There is no charge more frequent against the champions of dogmatic theology than that of imputing to the words of Scripture a meaning which they have only gathered in passing through the schools—in other words, of seeing the past by the light of the present. Yet is not this later negative criticism only an illustration in far more exaggerated form of the self-same tendency? for do we not here see not only the past read by the light of the present, but the Christ of the past ignored, and a modern Christ substituted in his room? Surely this is dogmatism of the wildest description; surely this is a desertion of that very canon of criticism which these men are so anxious to uphold, —the state of unbiased indifference in the examination of truth. To this extent, then, the revival of Rationalism represented by Schenkel and Renan has been tinged with the spirit of the mythical theory; in every other respect it belongs to the past. It is Rationalism softened down by its contact with Mythicism, yet it is only in the degree of its intensity that it differs from the Rationalism of the former age. When we hear even Renan saying, in relation to the person of Jesus, 'God was in him,' when we hear Schenkel speaking of Christ's character as a sinless one, we are forced, indeed, to confess, and to confess with gratitude, that we are no longer living in the atmosphere of Wegscheider and Paulus. But while we admit that Renan and Schenkel have been impelled by the influences of a higher age to make statements inconsistent with their own scepticism, we cannot close our eyes to the fact that the direction to which their efforts point is one not progressive, but retrogressive—not in the future, but in the past—not the product of their own age, but the relic and rejected garment of an age which has passed away.

Perhaps, in speaking of the modern attempts to rekindle the fire of Rationalism by applying to it the torch of Mythicism, we might have mentioned the name of one who is deservedly ranked amongst the first of biblical critics; we mean Ewald. His whole system is based upon the possibility of uniting the rationalistic and mythical standpoints; and this he endeavours to illustrate through the whole history of the Jewish people, in his very elaborate and remarkable work, *God in Israel*. If we have not given any prominence to the views of Ewald in these pages, it has not been from any depreciation of his writings, but because these writings are rather critical than theological. Nor are we sure that there is not in Ewald something which transcends the range either of Mythicism or of Rationalism. We rather think that Ewald must be classed amongst those who, while they have appropriated and blended many contrary opinions, are yet prepared to acknowledge a supernatural element in the history of Christianity. He is only brought into contact with the facts of the gospel in the concluding volume of his work. With these New Testament incidents, as with those of the old dispensation, he deals for the most part in a rather destructive manner, regarding some as mythical, some as admitting of a rationalistic interpretation, and some as combining the elements of both. Nevertheless it must be confessed, that amidst these undoubted traces of a negative bias there lurks a something deeper, which partakes of a character more favourable to the presence of a supernatural element in history. Of the character of Christ he speaks in a strain so exalted that one can hardly believe him to be contemplating a merely human ideal. Regarding the resurrection of Christ he gives a testimony which, in one so unbiased in favour of historical truth, amounts to a strong concession. Strauss had endeavoured to account for this fact by referring its origin to the subjective vision of St. Paul, recorded in his epistles; Paulus had endeavoured to account for it by the supposition that Christ was taken down from the cross while He was yet alive. Ewald, rejecting all attempts to explain it, accepts the great fact of the resurrection on the evidence of history, and declares that nothing can be more historical. Here we have certainly a return to something beyond either the mythical or the rational standpoint,—the recognition of an element in Christianity which mere nature cannot account for and human reason cannot explain. In this respect, therefore, Ewald may be regarded as a more direct opponent of Strauss than either Schenkel or Renan; for he admits into Christianity something which is older than the theories of Rationalism and Mythicism, and which cannot by any stretch of reasoning be made to harmonize with them.

Now let us just ask, Whence proceeds this want of

a settled basis in the ranks of negative criticism? The mythical theory of Strauss professed to account for the whole phenomena of Christianity by accepting its facts as the symbols of abstract ideas. That such a theory should be attacked by the orthodox is not surprising; but that it should be assailed by the opponents of orthodoxy is a very remarkable thing, and a circumstance which furnishes a strong presumption against the truth of the system. The fact that Renan, Schenkel, Ewald, Keim, and the large majority of those who have a prejudice against the supernatural in history, are yet not prepared to join in the solution which Strauss offers, but are forced backward upon a Rationalism which has been long dead and buried—that fact, we say, is peculiarly significant as to the position and influence of the mythical theory. It indicates, with an unerring voice, that this theory has failed to meet a special want of the human mind. Mythicism contemplates the nature of Man only in one of its aspects; it views him merely as a spiritual being, and forgets that he is after all but partially a spirit. We have been constituted not only with inward susceptibilities, but with relations to the outer world which cannot be ignored; and any system of philosophy or form of religious belief which closes its eyes to this fact will inevitably meet that dissolution which is the lot of one-sided views. It is on this account that the mythical theory has never been able to command the suffrages even of those who might naturally have been expected to support it; it is on this account that, while its life has been more brilliant, it has been far more brief than that of its predecessors. It came into the world as a new solution of difficulties and problems which had perplexed the mind of centuries. Its first appearance was startling in its effect, and the mind of Germany was dazzled by its lustre into forgetfulness of its real tendency. The very opposition it encountered from the defenders of the orthodox belief is an evidence that its earliest manifestation was received as a signal of danger. And yet this theory contained within itself the seeds of inevitable decay; and that decay has come much more through its own inherent weakness than as the result of those strokes inflicted upon it by its adversaries. Nay, strange to say, the finishing blow has been given by its own hand. Not Schenkel, not Renan, not Ewald, not the revival of Rationalism nor the reaction of orthodoxy has put the last touch upon the demolition of this system; it has come from Strauss himself—from the hand of that man who gave it birth, and who has latterly been its almost exclusive representative. The mythical theory has ended its days by suicide, and has given up in despair those conclusions and standpoints which at one time it regarded as the very elements of truth. To the exhibition of this final catastrophe we now briefly address ourselves.

CHAPTER XV.

'THE OLD FAITH AND THE NEW.'

SUCH is the title of that book which marks the latest product of extreme negative criticism. Its author is that same Strauss, who, nearly forty years before, had given forth to the world a theory which, in his opinion, would at once supersede and explain the existence of historical Christianity. But in these latter days he abandons that theory as itself belonging to an age which has gone by. What in the days of his youth he called the new faith, he has found to be itself old and ready to vanish; and without assuming any longer the attitude of one who seeks to inaugurate a school of religious belief, he reveals himself to the world in an aspect of pure negation, and boldly devotes himself to the work of theological destruction. He proposes these four questions, and proceeds to answer them:—Are we any longer Christians? Have we any longer a religion? What is our conception of the universe? and, What should be our rule of life? It is manifest that in order of thought the second of these questions should come first; for if we have no longer any religion, it will be in vain to inquire if we are any longer Christians. To this second and most comprehensive question Strauss does not in words give a definite answer; but his whole reasoning points to the conclusion that he regards religion, in the common sense of the term, as something which man has outgrown. In agreement with Schleiermacher, he defines religion to be the feeling of absolute dependence, but, unlike Schleiermacher, he intends the definition to be a disparagement of religion. He makes the feeling of absolute dependence identical with the sense of fear: Man perceives his own helplessness, and therefore looks for succour to something out of himself. But in this Strauss forgets that we ought to measure the value of a thing not by its lowest, but by its highest manifestation. Even if it be conceded that religion begins with the sense of absolute dependence, and the concession is by no means inevitable, it still remains an undeniable truth, that religion in its ultimate development grows into something deeper and far higher. We do not describe the attributes of a man by the aspect they would present in his childish years; we take them at their full standard, and judge of them at their best. Even so, in contemplating the nature of religion, it is surely neither fair nor philosophical to measure it by the infancy of its being, when it is manifest to the most common observation that this stage has long since been outgrown. Nor can it ever be proved that, even at its beginning, religion is nothing more than the sense of absolute dependence. Absolute dependence is indeed the occasion which calls it forth, just as the visible world is the occasion which calls forth the consciousness of life; but life is altogether different from the visible world, and religion may be altogether different from the dependence which first awakened it.

So also, when Strauss proceeds to examine one by one the doctrines of dogmatic theology, he manifests the same tendency to approach his subject with a foregone conclusion. When he rejects the belief in a Personal God, on the ground that modern science has disproved the idea of a throne beyond the stars, he takes it for granted that such a conception of Deity is inevitably bound up with the idea of His Personality —in other words, he assumes that the believer in a Personal God is constrained to think of Him as a Being who dwells outside the universe. Such a ridiculous assumption it would be equally ridiculous to waste time in refuting. Or when, again, in speaking of the doctrine of Immortality, Strauss labours to obliterate the essential distinction between matter and mind, on the ground that we could not conceive the co-existence of two such opposite essences, he manifestly ignores one important consideration, and it is this,— that if things so unlike can be conceived as identical, it is equally easy to conceive them as existing separately. It is neither our province nor our purpose to follow him in these efforts after theological destruction; our sole design in noticing his last work is to exhibit the final goal of negative criticism,—the legitimate conclusion to which the philosophy of the Left has conducted its adherents. We see Strauss begin by rejecting a historical in favour of a mythical Christianity, and end by abandoning the mythical Christ in favour of no Christ at all. If his answer to the first question is somewhat vague, that to the second is not for a moment doubtful. He boldly asserts that Christianity as a form of religious belief must now come to an end. On this head he revives most of the arguments against historical Christianity which he had adduced in his former work; yet his new faith is in advance of his old one. His previous attacks upon the gospel history had been designed to pave the way for the reception of a mythical Christ; but here the mythical and the historical are alike thrown overboard. The truth is, that this last work of negative criticism is not so much directed against any form of religion as against the idea of religion itself. Religion is here contemplated as something which involves an effete conception of the universe. It is looked upon as belonging to an age which was ignorant of scientific culture, and unconscious how nature was bound by the rigid chain of law; and it is called upon to retire into that past of which it is only a relic and a monument, and to leave the spirit of a new age to work out a higher faith. Nature is now to be viewed in an altogether different aspect; no longer as a piece of mechanism which has been constructed by a great artificer, nor yet even as an outward organism which has an inward personal soul, but as a grand system of forces, self-acting and self-originating, which are themselves only the correlations and manifestations of an unknown ultimate force underlying all. In the room of ecclesiastical dogma and Christian tradition we are to substitute the laboriously-attained results of researches into nature and history; and instead of occupying the practical life in the acceptance of dogmas alike unpractical and unreal, we should study those arts of poetry and music, which have an inherent tendency to produce culture and refinement.

Such is the new faith which Strauss proposes to substitute for the old. It has been frequently described as the profession of Materialism, but in truth it is not so; at least it is not so in the ancient sense of that word. It is the Materialism of Professor Huxley, of Stuart Mill, of Positivism in general. Strictly speaking, it has no more claim to the name of Materialism than it has to that of Spiritualism, for it regards matter and spirit as alike the appellations for unknown forces, or rather as only the names by which we designate two different manifestations of one great underlying force, itself uncomprehended and incomprehensible. But without assigning any name to this conception of the universe, it is interesting to remark that convergence of extremes to which we have already pointed as the goal of the Left Hegelianism. We have seen this philosophy approaching the problem of human life from a standpoint of Spiritualism so high that even the interests of the individual man were regarded by it as nothing. We have seen it claiming for the human spirit all the prerogatives of divinity, and refusing to admit the possibility of a

God transcending humanity. We have seen it rejecting historical records, in so far as they are any more than parables of spiritual truth, and in the professed interest of our spiritual nature reducing the gospel to an allegory. We see it now, through the very excess of its own strength, meeting side by side with that physical standpoint which had its origin in a precisely opposite source, and finding itself in union with those very conclusions of English empiricism which it had been the special object of this philosophy to reject and avoid.

Are we, then, to believe that this new faith promulgated by Strauss is to be the ultimate goal of the religious spirit of Germany? We cannot do so. So far, indeed, as present appearances go, it would seem as if this new faith had scarcely a rival in the field. It is frequently averred that the Hegelian theology has been extinguished in Germany; and the utterance is made with triumph. The statement is undoubtedly true; but whether it be a matter of congratulation will be judged differently by different minds. If the Hegelian theology be dead, it has not yielded up its life to any system which claims the name of orthodox, but, on the contrary, has surrendered to one which expressly rejects the religious standpoint. At the present moment this so-called new faith has far more adherents in Germany than the mythical theory ever had; and the only adversary which seeks to dispute its possession is that theology of Schleiermacher, whose tenets are so vague, or rather so all-comprehending, that they might even be made to include within their pale the disciples of the new faith themselves. If, therefore, we look at present appearances, we might be tempted to conclude that this new faith would be the final one. But the spirit of philosophy forbids us to do so. We have seen that the Hegelian theology itself prepared us for a period of great negation preceding an age of perfect reconstruction; and surely here negation has reached that limit beyond which it can go no farther. The new faith of Strauss is one which is reached by giving exclusive prominence to a single side of human nature, and contemplating that side as if it were the whole man. Undoubtedly Man is a scientific being; he has been created with a tendency to abstract and generalize, to examine his own thoughts, and refer them to their legitimate laws. Undoubtedly any religious belief which is incapable of accommodation to this part of our nature is not perfectly adapted to the wants of the human soul; and therefore a faith which would be abiding must be able to become scientific. But while all this is true, it is not the whole truth. There is another side of human nature, equally prominent, and even more frequently exhibited,—a part of our being which is quite removed from abstraction and generalization and scientific reasoning, but which yet claims no inconsiderable share in the search for truth in every department; we mean that side of our being which is commonly comprehended under the name of intuition. Intuitions are not scientific, because they are incapable of proof; but they are themselves the basis of all science, and are presupposed as the foundations of every speculative argument. When, therefore, Strauss declares the new faith to be the laboriously-attained results of scientific investigation, he forgets altogether those objects of belief which are not laboriously attained at all, but are reached by a flash of intuitive consciousness. Even Comte was compelled, in the interests of Positive science, to give a place to the dictates of these intuitions. He perceived that if a system would be scientific, it must deal with all the facts of the case; and as the instinct of worship was as permanently discernible as the tendency to analysis, he was constrained to make religion an integral part of his Positive philosophy. In this respect the Frenchman has for once been more far-sighted than the German. Strauss contemplates Man purely as an intellectual machine, as a being whose province in this world is only to observe and combine. He entirely overlooks the fact, which was once the very leading principle of German theology, that Man brings to the world as much as he gets from it, and is himself something more than the objects he analyses. The new faith of Strauss is therefore a one-sided faith,—a faith which can only exist so long as Man is viewed in antagonism with himself; and as such a view of human nature is itself not capable of enduring, it may be confidently predicted, that the faith of which it is the foundation and support will vanish before a more comprehensive survey of those elements which constitute the basis of human nature.

CHAPTER XVI.

PARALLEL BETWEEN THE HISTORY OF ENGLISH AND GERMAN THEOLOGY.

THERE is more contained in the whole than in all the parts taken together, and in contemplating a system in the entire range of its history, there may be gathered some conclusions which did not appear in the analysis of its fragments. We have in the preceding chapters given a brief sketch of the different phases which German theology has exhibited from the end of last century to the present time. We are now in a position to view it no longer in relation to its parts merely, but as a grand unity, presenting in the union of all its parts a distinct manifestation of the human intellect. It is now that for the first time we are entitled to ask, What is the relation of the theology of Germany to our own modes of religious thought? Does it present to us any point of contact? Does it supply any object of interest to the English student? We have already said that the starting-point of English and German thought is radically different, the former being empirical, the latter supersensuous. But while there is manifestly a decided contrast in standpoint

English and German Theology. 173

observable at every stage, there is discernible at the conclusion of all the stages a not less remarkable historical resemblance. Strange to say, the theology of these two nations, starting as it does from so different a base, has yet experienced in its progress nearly the same stages of external fortune; and as this fact alone is calculated to furnish a bond of mutual sympathy, it may not be altogether uninteresting to offer a brief sketch of that historical parallel which unites the diverse systems of religious thought. In the introduction to this subject we have already pointed out how Germany, during the Middle Ages, presented a reaction against the Roman hierarchy in those efforts after personal communion with God which pass by the name of Mysticism. In offering this reaction to the hierarchy, Germany presents her first point of contact to the theology of England. It may be confidently affirmed, that in neither of these countries did the hierarchy ever find a congenial soil, in neither of them was it able to take permanent root, and in both of them it was opposed by repeated and violent revolutions. No doubt even at this early stage the difference of their theological standpoint made itself known. The Mysticism of Tauler and Ruysbroeck stands altogether apart from the practical tendencies of Wickliffe and the Lollards; but they are united in this, that they are both in search of the grand principle of personal liberty, and both opposed to authority as the ultimate basis of truth. Nor is it surprising that these nations which exhibited the earliest reactions should have been the foremost in that remarkable movement of the sixteenth century which we call the Reformation; it was only natural that the earliest preparation should produce the earliest fruit. In this religious revolution Germany took the lead by a few years; England was in this instance the follower. Yet she could not be called the imitator; for the movements were not only independent of each other, but in one sense proceeded from different sources,—that of Germany being purely theological, that of England in great measure political. Here, again, the one feature which united them was the protest for liberty. And not less remarkable is the fact, that these nations, which were so united in this revival of religious life, were fated almost simultaneously to pass through a stage of spiritual declension. It is a matter of history, that ere a century had passed away, the Church of Luther had already declined from that fresh and fervid piety which had constituted the glory of the Reformation era; justification by faith had become justification by *the* faith, and the assent to lifeless dogmas had taken the place of individual trust. It is equally notorious that almost at the same hour the Church of England was making a regress back to those elements which she had abandoned,—not, indeed, as in the case of Germany, by a return to dogmatism, but, in consistency with her own empirical tendency, by the attempt to re-establish an infallible Church. To both nations the declension brought disaster; and although their errors were different, they resulted in the same disaster—Rationalism. The infallibility of dogma and the infallibility of an outward Church were alike strenuously resisted by the natural reason of Man; and in this instance natural reason was in conformity with that spirit of the Reformation which was founded on the protest for individual liberty. In each case the progress of Rationalism was downwards. We have seen how in Germany it began as the ally of Christianity, then attempted to prune away from Christianity whatever could not be comprehended in itself, and finally revealed itself in the attitude of one claiming to be an independent source of divine knowledge. We have seen that it proceeded from subordinationism to Arianism, from Arianism to Socinianism, from Socinianism to the denial of the sinless humanity, and thence to a stage beyond Deism itself,—that so-called Illuminism, the offspring of the French Revolution, which denied the possibility of God. And if we turn to England, we shall find precisely the same stages of downward development. We there see Rationalism pitching its camp amongst the very defenders of Christianity, and manifesting its existence in the very form of their apologies, thereby virtually conceding the point that there is nothing in the religion of Christ which is not commensurate with human reason. We next see it separating itself from the camp of orthodoxy, and seeking, as in Germany, to modify the doctrines of the gospel into harmony with its own requirements, advancing by ever-increasing shades from the concealed Arianism of a Clarke to the avowed Arianism of a Whitby; then, with Priestley and Belgham, to the profession of entire Socinianism; and finally, in strict parallel with her Teutonic sister, to the open rupture with all forms of religion whatsoever. Rationalism, in both cases the inevitable result of those abuses which attended the exclusive predominance of authority, became itself in both cases the cause of abuses more heinous still, and so prepared the way for its own fall.

In the midst of this Rationalism there arose, in the very heart of England and Germany, a remarkable religious movement, whose professed object was to counteract it. In England it was called Methodism, in Germany it was named Pietism. In each country it manifested itself with such characteristic shades of difference as we should expect from the diverse nature of their soil. The enthusiasm of a Wesley, a Whitefield, and a Harris, springing as it did from a purely theological source, was altogether unfettered by the limits of intellectual speculation; the Pietism of a Bengel and an Oetinger was unable thus to separate itself from the results of scientific investigation, and strove to incorporate its existence with the culture of surrounding systems. But while Pietism and Methodism thus exhibited the shades peculiar to their nations, there was beneath these shades an underlying unity, which made them one parallel movement of religious life. They were both directed against the same tendency. They opposed alike the Rationalism which would reduce Christianity to a product of nature, and the formalism which had eaten away the very life of the orthodox Church. They both designed to substitute for barren forms a fresh, life-giving spirit,—a vitality which would make itself felt and known by the energy which it would awaken,—a fervour which would surround the visible Church with an atmosphere of moral earnestness. Unfortunately they thereby placed themselves in antagonism to that very orthodox Church which it was their design to vivify. The saints of to-day were the heretics of yesterday. The men to whose deeds we look back with gratitude and veneration, and whom we truly regard as the reformers of their age, have in every case been regarded by that age itself as only the disturbers of tranquillity and the contrivers of innovation. In England and in Germany alike, the orthodox Church of the eighteenth century was a Church which had no sympathy with the enthusiasm of religious zeal, and which looked upon the efforts after a more intense vitality with that aristocratic contempt with which the observer of rigid etiquette regards the outbursts of spontaneous nature. Yet, misplaced as that contempt was, the very fact of its existence paralyzed the influence of these religious reactions. Pietism and Methodism would have exercised a powerful effect in checking the progress of Rationalism had they been recognised as the allies of orthodoxy; but as, in relation to the orthodox Church, they were themselves in nearly the same condemnation with the system they opposed, they were compelled to struggle with all those disadvantages which follow the adherents of a party, and were exposed to imputations and suspicions which prevented the seed which they sowed from taking root in the soil.

Accordingly it was fated that neither Pietism in Germany nor Methodism in England should be that method by which Rationalism should be overthrown, but that her destruction should come from her own ranks, and be inflicted by her own armour. The incompetence of reason must be established by reason herself, and philosophy itself must refute the claims it had made to an absolute knowledge. In England and in Germany, Rationalism came forth with a weapon in her hand to inflict self-destruction, and what Methodism and Pietism had failed to do was accomplished by her own self-upbraidings. Two men appeared upon the stage as the special representatives of this work; the one was David Hume, the other Emanuel Kant. Both had received one mission to fulfil, although in the accomplishment of that mission their designs were very different. Hume attacked Rationalism with an unsparing hand, and levelled with the dust the structures which had been reared by the pride of Man; but he did so only in order that he might rest amidst the ruins, and exist in freedom from that responsibility which belongs to the possession of knowledge; he destroyed Man's belief in himself that he might establish an absolute scepticism. Kant also attacked Rationalism with a keen and penetrating logic, and demolished one by one the citadels she had pronounced impregnable; but he did so not that he might rest amidst the ruins, but that from the depth of these ruins he might construct a brighter edifice. We have seen, however, that while the destruction succeeded, the reconstruction failed, and therefore the German philosopher must rank with his English contemporary as one of those whose mission it was to be apostles of destruction. The sequel of German theology is a long attempt to fill up that gulf between the natural and the supernatural which was left by the Kantian deluge. We see Schlegel flying back for refuge to the bosom of that Romanism which the Reformation had left behind; Fichte flying inwards to the bosom of that Cartesianism which began by seeking a refuge in the human soul itself; Schleiermacher seeking to reconcile the natural and the supernatural by reducing religion to a feeling of the heart alone; Hegel and Schelling arriving at a more real reconstruction by finding the basis of truth in the very contradictions that environ it. Then, by one of those unaccountable perversities, we see German theology deserting for a time the results of her own development, and proceeding step by step to abandon those conclusions which she had attained with such research and labour. In Kant we have the struggles of her birth, in Fichte the helplessness of her infancy, in Schleiermacher the imagination of her youth, in Hegel the reflectiveness of her manhood; with him she reaches the summit of the hill, and thenceforth her progress hitherto has been only a descent into the valleys.

And what has been the sequel of English theology? Hume, like Kant, destroyed Rationalism, and since the days of Hume, Rationalism rarely has appeared; the orthodox Church herself has abandoned the attempt to demonstrate the existence of light, and Paley may be regarded as the last of our apologists. The immediate effect, indeed, of this fall of Rationalism was to paralyze historical development; for in England, as in Germany, it left between the human and the divine a great chasm to be filled. This nineteenth century had already opened ere the speculative tendency began again to manifest itself in our island; but when it did appear, it came, as in Germany, with a variety of aspects, which was alone a proof of the freshness of its life. On the one side there was a regressive movement into the haven of an infallible Church, where the human mind might cut the knot of its difficulties by appeal to an outward authority. On the other side there was a bias leaning rather to the negative aspect of things, and more eager to throw away the chaff than to collect the wheat. Between these tendencies there has arisen in England, as in Germany, a third and intermediate party, avoiding the extremes of both, and in one sense uniting the advantages of each; and it is from this quarter that most of all we look for such a revival of theology in England as shall at once express the fervour of religious zeal and blend with it the culture of scientific progress. Moreover, the spirit of science itself has in our country assumed an aspect which might be called semi-theological. There is no expression more frequently heard than the phrase English Materialism; and yet it is a truth which

English and German Theology. 181

cannot be too strongly emphasized, that the Materialism of England in the nineteenth century is no longer the Materialism of the England of a hundred years ago. If to the eye of modern British science nature does not present the aspect of a spiritual existence, it just as little exhibits the features of a dead material organism. More and more is the scientific spirit awakening to the perception that there is something in the universe beneath what eye has seen or ear has heard; more and more is it realizing the presence of a Force, all-embracing, unseen, inscrutable, persistent everywhere,—a Force of which all other forces are but the diverse manifestations, and in which all the rivers of life move and have their being. We do not say that in calling such a Being by the name of force British science has fixed upon the most happy, the most reverential appellation. We do not say that by such a name she does not manifest her wonted predilection for the physical over the moral; but we do say that this conception of the scientific spirit is already in advance of Materialism. We have seen that here at last the German and the English mind seem to have found a meeting-place; but we must never forget, that what to Germany is a fall is to England a rise. The spirits of the two nations have come into contact not more by the stooping of the one than by the elevation of the other. It is a notorious fact, that at the present moment the theology of Hegel has more admirers in Oxford than in Berlin; it is a notorious fact, that the original life of German philosophy, which has deserted the home of its nativity, is to be found occasionally in all its vigour bursting forth on British soil. And now that at length the partial declension of the German spirit from its first ideal standpoint, and the partial emancipation of our own from its first material envelopment, have mutually contributed to furnish a common ground of operation, are we not entitled to hope that the freshness of the life which is rising may transfuse its energy into the life which is waning, and that England may give back to Germany that speculative vigour which she derived from German soil?[1]

[1] See supplementary note, page 212.

SUPPLEMENTARY NOTES.

INTRODUCTION.—PAGE 2.

WE have called Mysticism an anticipation of the Protestant reaction. In doing so, we are far from asserting with Ullmann that the Mystics were the direct forerunners of the Lutheran theology. There was one point, indeed, which they held in common with Protestantism, and in opposition to Romanism, and that was the religious rights of the individual man. Romanism magnified the collective Church, and valued the individual only as a member of that Church. The Church was the sole medium of revelation, and it was only through the united body of believers that God would speak to the world. Against this one-sided tendency Mysticism and Protestantism alike protested; both sought to vindicate the importance of each separate soul, both vehemently struggled to defend the possibility of a personal communion with God. But here their similarity ended and their difference began. Mysticism regarded the communion of the soul with God as an already established fact; Protestantism looked upon it as something to come. Mysticism started from the thought that God is naturally in union with each human spirit; Protestantism took its stand upon the principle that God is by nature separated from the heart of every man. Mysticism declared the beginning of salvation to be justification by the divine life; Protestantism made the corner-stone of religion justification by faith. In Mysticism there is no obstacle experienced to the realization of personal purity: we have only to fix our thoughts on God to receive an influx of the divine nature; hence Ruysbroek speaks of the spirit imbibing directly the brightness of God, and becoming the very brightness which it imbibes. But in Protestantism the divine life cannot be possessed by Man as a gift of nature; there is a disturbing element to be overcome, and that is sin. Before we can even touch the threshold of the life of God, we must be made to feel that the partition wall has been broken down, and that heaven and earth have been reconciled. Justification has thus a totally different meaning with Luther and Calvin, from what it bears with Tauler and Ruysbroek; with the former it is the sense of restoration to divine favour, with the latter it is the actual possession of God within the soul. The indwelling of the Divine Spirit in both cases is recognised as the essence of salvation; but with the Mystic this indwelling is the beginning of all, can be reached in a flash of intuition, or attained in a moment of contemplation; with the Protestant it is an inheritance which has been purchased with blood and tears and pain, and can only be appropriated through a sacrifice which has broken the enmity of earth and heaven.

CHAPTER II.—PAGE 24.

THE analogy between this part of the Kantian philosophy and the corresponding portion of the Augustinian theology is indeed very marked. It is not, of course, wonderful that it should be so. The earliest centuries of Christian history are in strict union with the highest philosophy. The Christianity of that age had not yet divorced itself from worldly culture, had not yet attempted to draw a line of demarcation between the secular and the sacred. On the contrary, she regarded all earthly streams as her tributaries, and was not ashamed to be fed by the confluence of mundane waters. In Augustine we behold the struggle between the old and the new, between that epoch when Christianity claimed philosophy as her handmaid, and that time when she began to exalt herself over human nature; yet it seems to us, that in the heart of Augustine the old ever dominated the new, and the claims of philosophic culture outweighed the claims of ecclesiastical tradition. To Augustine, as to Kant, the highest freedom is not the exercise of individual will, but the very subordination of that will to the duties and requirements of an absolute morality. He tells us that man was never created free, in the sense of being undetermined between good and evil; that, on the contrary, he sprang from the hand of his Creator in union with the *heart* of his Creator, with a will already biased towards God, and already bent towards virtue. He had received, indeed, what no other creature had received, the power of choice between right and wrong; but according to Augustine, it was his duty not to use that power. He quotes with singular felicity that verse, 'I have set before thee life and death, therefore choose life,' and he argues from this that Man's possession of the power of choice was itself the temptation, that here was the first forbidden fruit on which he was called to close his eyes. He had the choice of life and death, but he was not therefore to choose between them; a man only chooses between equal things, and death is not comparable with life. The moment he began to choose he began to fall, for in that act he placed upon an equal level two motives which have no natural equality, the love of goodness and the love of self. Nay, from the very fact that Man had originally the power of choice, Augustine will not concede that his first paradise was the highest conceivable glory. He distinguishes three kinds of liberty. The first is liberty to choose between good and evil, which was the gift of unfallen Man. The second is liberty to choose evil, but not to follow goodness, which is the condition of Man in his fallen state. The third is liberty to choose goodness, but not to follow evil, which is destined to be the ultimate state of the redeemed in heaven. Here the highest manifestation of freedom is declared to be the condition of a soul so completely wedded to virtue, that the possibility of loving vice cannot even present itself as an alternative; and in this the early theologian is in singular agreement with the modern German philosopher. Nor is the analogy between them less apparent when we pass to consider the nature of the Fall itself. It is well known that Augustine regarded sin in the first instance as simply a separation from God; it consisted, according to him, in the life of the soul endeavouring to set up its own individual being as an ultimate principle; this is the real philosophic significance of what in the moral sphere is called selfishness. And we need not point out to the student how entirely this view harmonizes with the Kantian theory,—a theory which professes to ground all moral delinquency in the predominance of self-love, in the efforts of individual men to hold their interests apart from universal Man. Indeed, if the student would understand this portion of the Kantian philosophy, he cannot do better than read and carefully ponder the corresponding portion of the Augustinian theology. He will find in both many points of contact, many traces of a kindred spirit. In both he will see the efforts of a mind to reconstruct the fabric of its faith upon the ruins of those beliefs which it has weighed in the balance and found wanting. In both he will meet the same Platonic contempt for the outer world, as something incongruous with the divine life. In both he will find the same desire to merge individual existence in the life of a great community or visible church; only with Augustine it was the church of the Roman hierarchy, with Kant it was the ideal church of the future. Shall we add one parallel more? In both he shall discover the same inconsistency, the same tendency to go back to those elements they have surmounted. Kant in his moral argument unconsciously seeks to revive the Rationalism he has destroyed, and Augustine, in his devotion to an ecclesiastical empire, tends under the guise of church authority to resuscitate that world-power which his philosophy had declared to be alien to true religion.

PAGE 26.

The statement that authority is destructive to morality exhibits a contradiction in the Kantian system; what he means is, that an *outward* authority is destructive to morality. It is well known that he did not regard authority in the abstract as having this tendency, for he calls conscience the categorical imperative, that is to say, the power which speaks with a command so absolute and so unqualified that there can be no appeal from its decision. It would seem, then, that even in the view of Kant, authority may become not only free from antagonism to morality, but itself the source of all moral impressions; it only requires to be translated from the region of outward life into the inward region of the heart. Is it not, however, natural to ask if there may not exist a congruity between even an outward authority and an inward perception? Does a command emanating from without of necessity prove

Supplementary Notes.

destructive to the spontaneous instincts of the soul? May it not rather corroborate them, endorse them, confirm them? The question opens up one of the most keenly debated problems in the whole sphere of ethics. What is the ground of moral obligation? is a question which lies at the root both of philosophy and of religion, and it has by no means been answered with unanimous agreement. One school, to which Kant belongs, places our obligation to do right entirely in the nature of things. Man is here a law to himself. Another school, which numbers amongst its votaries that large party of medieval theologians called Nominalists, finds the ground of our obedience to duty to consist entirely in the absolute will of the Supreme Being; and to such an extent is this carried, that Duns Scotus is not afraid to affirm, that if God should so command it, vice would become virtue. Is there any necessity to adopt either of these extremes, or rather does not the truth lie in something which is common to both? May we not hold that morality has its source in the will of a Supreme Being, and yet hold that this divine will is the expression of a divine character? May we not believe that we are impelled to follow virtue by the nature of virtue herself, and yet acknowledge that the nature of virtue is nothing else than the nature of God, and that which prompts the will of God? What do we suppose to be that authority which Christianity claims as an outward revelation? Is it something which addresses merely the eye or the ear, or which speaks only to the impulses of fear within us? Assuredly not. The only authority to which the Christian religion would attach the slightest value is just that categorical imperative which Kant so eulogizes. If its command comes from without, it speaks only to that which is within; if it is uttered from the flames of Sinai, it is written on the tables of the heart; if it is expressed in forms which are intelligible to the perception of external sense, it is immediately translated by the soul into something which eye hath not seen nor ear heard. The power of Christianity, the only power which it will consent to wield, is the demonstration of the spirit, and it reaches its highest glory when it has succeeded in commending itself to every man's conscience. An authority from without need not be an outward authority, need not be foreign to the soul. The commands of Christianity certainly come from a source which is without us, in so far as they proceed from a height which is higher than we; but whenever these commands have come into contact with our spirits, we find in them something which is commensurate with our highest being, in union with our deepest selves, and powerful chiefly as a lever and incentive to lift us into the fruition of our noblest aspirations.

CHAPTER VI.—PAGE 77.

IN applying the word *atheism* to the system of Fichte, we are far from asserting that Fichte was himself an atheist; he was accused of this in his own lifetime, and he vehemently denied it. It has frequently been remarked that there is a wonderful dualism between the systems and the lives of philosophers. It has not seldom happened, that a man whose philosophic creed has seemed to point in a direction unfavourable to piety, has yet possessed himself a sincerely pious soul. Such a man was Benedict Spinoza; his system has generally been regarded as opposed to all religious orthodoxy, but his life was singularly pure in an age of much impurity, and Schleiermacher is not afraid to say, in the zeal of fervent admiration, that he was full of the Holy Ghost. And such a man, too, we believe to have been Fichte; pious, reverent, religious, self-denying, in a certain sense even prayerful. Those attributes which his philosophy tore away from the conception of God were given back to it by the instincts of his heart; the man was no atheist, though the result of his reasoning was atheistic. But as we are dealing here not with men but with their systems, we cannot allow our estimate of their characters to blind us to the errors of their philosophy. We believe Fichte to have been a more pious man than either Schelling or Hegel, but we must confess that the religious creed of Fichte is far less reverent than Schelling or Hegel's creed. Whatever Fichte may have felt in his heart, it is unquestionable that in his reasoning he denies the personality of God; nay, he not merely denies this personality, but he maintains such a conception to be logically impossible; his formula is this, an absolute personality is a contradiction in terms. Now this formula has, since the days of Fichte, been repeated and reverberated in many different quarters, and has not seldom been allowed to wield the authority of an axiom which must dispense with all further argument. It is only right, therefore, that the student should calmly and carefully consider whether there be or be not any grounds for this dictum, and we shall endeavour briefly to lay before him what seems to us to be the just inference on this subject.

When it is said that an absolute personality is a contradiction in terms, our first inquiry ought to be as to the meaning of the terms in question; what is meant by personality, and what is meant by absolute. Now it so happens that the word personality has a totally different sense in popular conception to that which it bears in philosophic thought. The word in its common use is intended to designate the possession of a certain bodily shape. We need not say that in this popular view the statement of Fichte is incontrovertible. The very idea of a bodily shape implies limitation. That which has a figure is by its very nature bounded in particular directions, marked off from other things by specific limits, and wrought into symmetry by adjustment into definite proportions. To speak, therefore, of a shape or figure so gigantic as to have neither beginning nor end, is as great a contradiction as to say that two and two make five; in this sense an absolute or infinite personality is indeed an impossible thought. But this is manifestly not the true meaning of the word personality. If the student will turn to our exposition of the Hegelian Trinity, he will find that we have there endeavoured to exhibit the essence of personality not as mere bodily shape, but as self-consciousness, which includes within itself alike the soul and the body; and if he consider the dictum of Fichte in the light of this higher definition, he will see that all contradiction has melted away. An absolute personality now becomes a perfect self-consciousness, a realizing of the fulness of existence to the utmost possible height of intensity. In this view, also, it will be found that the term absolute has undergone a similar change of meaning. In Germany it is used as equivalent to infinite; and although in our country Hamilton and Mansel have endeavoured to distinguish between them, there seems no just reason to adopt their distinction. Now, in our chapter on the school of Tübingen, we have tried to point out that there are two distinct meanings of the word infinite, and these will find a fitting application in the two senses we have given to the term personality. In the former sense, an absolute or infinite personality is a figure without boundaries, unbeginning, unending, incapable of being measured with the eye either of sight or of imagination, and therefore unable to be conceived at all: in other words, a contradiction in terms. In the latter sense, an absolute or infinite personality is a being who entirely and fully realizes his own existence, and every power of whose mind is exercised in the highest intensity. It is perfectly clear that in this view the infinitude of God, so far from being a barrier to His personality, is the very thing which renders that personality complete; nay, in this light there is no being in the universe so personal as God, for the very reason that He alone is absolute. Man has not an absolute self-consciousness, and therefore he has not an absolute personality. We only know ourselves by knowing others, and our personality thus comes to us as if it were a gift derived from experience; the divine self-consciousness is alone independent of external influences, and therefore it is there alone that we can find the exercise of a purely personal power; and the manifestation of a purely spiritual life. These are the grounds on which we are compelled to reject the formula of Fichte. Like every theory which has numbered many votaries, it has undoubtedly a side of truth. It strikes at a common and, we think, a very erroneous conception of the Deity, and its stroke is not unerring nor its aim unsuccessful. But its main use must lie in exposing the error of that view which it assails, and in leading the mind to another and a higher view. The dictum of Fichte has only succeeded in proving that there is a gross material conception of God, which in the very thinking of it we are forced to abandon; the inevitable and desirable result must be to direct us to those spiritual views of truth which shall be free from the irreverence of contradiction, and unaffected by the mutation of outward forms.

CHAPTER VII.—Page 85.

THERE are gropings after Hegelianism, just as there are gropings after Christianity, as far back as the dawn of speculation. The oldest attempt in the world to formulate religious ideas into a systematic theology is, so far as known to us, the creed of Brahminism. That this creed, like every other form of faith, had both a popular and a philosophical interpretation, it is impossible to doubt. We are told by many writers that the three objects of Indian worship, Brahma, Vishnu, and Shiva, constituted not so much a trinity as a triad; not one god in three persons, but three persons, each of whom was a god; and we have no doubt whatever, that in the opinion of the uncultured mass this belief was the current one. But it is admitted by all competent authorities, that the philosophic minds of India attached a purely spiritual significance to these three divine personages; a significance which, while it preserved their distinctions, tended at the same time to reduce them into unity. Nothing, we think, can more clearly illustrate this than the metaphor under which the Brahmins themselves endeavour to describe their threefold deity. Brahma corresponds to the first person; and he is likened to a boundless ocean, without beginning and without end, shoreless, fathomless, limitless. Then we are asked to imagine that in the lapse of long ages a few drops of this ocean's spray are cast off from its mighty bosom, and fall, as it were by accident, 'into a bottle.' In this narrow prison-house these stray drops of the great divine life are shut up for centuries, and that which had no boundary finds a body to contain it. At last in the fulness of time the bottle breaks, and the imprisoned life is set free, free to go back again into the bosom of that ocean which has been its eternal home. Now the whole of this imagery is very striking and suggestive. Let the student just compare it with the account we have given of the evolution of the Hegelian Trinity in time, and he will be struck with the similarity which the speculations of antiquity present to those of modern civilisation. In the Trinity of Hegel we have the same three divine movements which are indicated in the creed of Brahminism, except that perhaps the transition from a poetic to a scientific age has lent more logical exactitude to his statements and expressions, coupled always with the fact that Christianity has given a new application to every theory. In their outlines, however, Hegelianism and Brahminism are allied. Hegelianism, like Brahminism, starts with the boundless ocean of divine being spreading itself forth without beginning and without end; a life which we cannot even conceive, because there exist no landmarks by which we can define its position. Here again, as in the creed of the Brahmin, we have something which exactly corresponds to the spray-drops falling into the bottle, for we find that this divine life eventually limits itself by the very act of creation, and surrounds itself with that body or dwelling-place to which we give the name of nature. Here, too, the dwelling-place becomes at last a prison-house, and separates the life enclosed within it from that wider life which the prison walls are unable to cover; the spray-drops are divided from the eternal ocean. And here, in strict analogy with the same old philosophy, the bottle at length breaks into fragments; the imprisoned drops of divine life which we call humanity burst forth from the precincts of external nature, and, overleaping the barriers of sense, rush back again into the consciousness of their eternal origin, finding at once their freedom and their rest on the bosom of the infinite sea. Thus over the long centuries the philosophers of India and of Germany have shaken hands and declared themselves agreed. Many a pious Christian, who has never heard of the philosophers either of India or of Germany, has found a strange attraction in the old Brahminical metaphor,—and we catch something of the thoughts of long ago when we hear the modern worshipper of Christ expressing his desire, in the words of Keble, 'to lose himself in the ocean of His love.'

If we turn now to Platonism, we shall find that the highest philosophy of Greece singularly corresponds with the philosophy of ancient India. Here too we have a Trinity, and here too it is a Hegelian Trinity. The three terms which express it are the *On*, the *Psuche*, and the *Nous*. The *On* is the divine life in itself, in its boundlessness, its unbeginningness, its endlessness; it is the ocean without the shore. The *Psuche* is that portion of the divine life which has been imprisoned in nature, enclosed in the limits of a narrow cell, within whose walls it frets, and chafes, and struggles to be free. The *Nous* is the *Psuche* liberated; it is the imprisoned spray bursting the bottle and regaining its ocean home. Platonism is thus in many aspects the true child of Brahminism, as it is the true ancestor of Hegelianism. Nor need we pause to show that in that subsequent revival of the Platonic creed which permeates the Christian literature of the first three centuries, we find a reappearance of the same distinctive features. Every student knows how the Gnostics recognised a threefold life of God: there was first the divine existence in its fulness, confined within no dwelling-place, and inhabiting no form; there was next that existence in its imprisonment, shut up within the bodies of angels, and eventually enclosed in the limits of a human soul; and last of all, there was the great process of liberation, by which the divine life escaped from its enthralment and returned once more to the fulness of its being. And in these early Christian· systems there appears with peculiar prominence the idea of a trinity in Man. Man is conceived as having a threefold nature, or rather as being himself a compound of two natures. The Pneuma or spirit is the personality itself, that which constitutes us human beings. But this Pneuma or spirit of Man is not a simple idea; it includes two other ideas under it, for it implies both a body and a life. Neither a life without a body nor a body without a life would make a living personality, in other words, a human spirit; it is only when these are united that there comes forth, as the result of their union, a being to whose attributes and qualities we can attach the notion of personality. Such is the idea of a triune existence as it appears in the systems of Gnosticism, and the student who has read these pages cannot fail to be impressed with the close similarity which it presents to the idea of a Trinity as conceived by Hegel. But what shall be our inference from this impression? Shall we say with some that it proves Hegel to have been a plagiarist, or with others that his system is vitiated by the fact that the same thought was conceived in very old days? Either of these conclusions would scarcely be fair. On the one hand, Hegel claimed to be no more than every man of science claims to be,—an interpreter and expounder of the laws of nature; and in the exhibition of these laws he can hardly be accused of plagiarism. On the other hand, the Hegelians themselves might employ the very same facts as a source of strength to their own theory; they might contend that truth is ever old, and that the prevalence of these views in periods so distant and so various was a strong presumptive evidence of the soundness of their faith. Dogmatism on such a point is of course out of the question; errors and truths have alike a tendency to reproduce themselves from age to age, and it would be as unsafe as it would be unscientific to form on either side any strong preliminary judgment. We have placed before the student this prevalence of the Hegelian theory with a far different motive than that of prepossessing the mind in favour of its truth; our design in this has chiefly been to demonstrate its importance as a key to the world's religious history. It is not too much to say, that there will not be found one age of that history which is altogether free from traces of this doctrine's influence. Brahminism, Platonism, Alexandrianism, Gnosticism, the Mysticism of the pseudo-Dionysius in the fifth century, the speculations of Scotus Erigena in the ninth, the three ages of power, wisdom, and goodness delineated by the anti-papists of the thirteenth, and the protracted mystical reaction against Romanism which tinges the whole current of medieval days, are all more or less the foreshadowings and the anticipations of the transcendental philosophy of Germany in the nineteenth century. And if it be so, if Hegelianism can point to so many forerunners in the past, there is one conclusion which cannot be avoided; not certainly the truth of the theory,—that must be determined on other grounds,—but the advantage of knowing it as a means of historical research. From its prevalence in past ages we will not be warranted to infer that it is a true theology, but we will be abundantly entitled to conclude that, be it false or true, it is the key to many theologies, and the interpreter of many philosophies whose meaning must otherwise be lost in inexplicable mystery.

PAGE 86.

It may be asked, leaving altogether out of view the personal opinion of Hegel, What is the tendency of the Hegelian system in relation to the belief in immortality. The student who has discriminated the difference between the Right and the Left will at once perceive that our view on this subject will probably depend upon which of these explanations we adopt. He will see that the Right Hegelianism tends in an eminent degree to foster our sense of the soul's value, and therefore to confirm our faith in its immortality. On the other hand, he will be equally conscious that the Left Hegelianism has by nature the opposite tendency, because in this system the individual is contemplated only as a vanishing point, and the parts are lost in the whole. This, we say, is its natural tendency; yet it is by no means its universal result. Strauss and Baur belonged at one time to the same school. Both were men of the highest talents, and both thoroughly understood the logical consequences of their own speculations; yet, while Strauss rejected the belief in a personal immortality, there is reason to believe, from private testimony, that Baur retained it. The truth is, that no form of pantheism, however gross, is of necessity destructive to the hope of futurity. The popular opinion is, that according to the pantheist the souls of men at death are absorbed into the soul of the universe. But what the pantheist does hold is, not that the souls of men will be one with God at death, but that they are one with Him in life,—that at this present moment they are so intimately a part of the divine nature, that death itself could add nothing to the union. And might not the pantheist argue thus: 'Is not my view compatible with immortality? We are now one with God, and yet we have not lost our sense of identity. The mere fact of death cannot bring us nearer to the Infinite, and what reason is there to believe that it should take away from us that individual life which we already possess?' Nor can we say that in thus reasoning the pantheist would be altogether illogical. If at this moment we are united to God so closely as to be essentially one with Him, if the union be of such a nature that no soul in the universe can be regarded as outside the divine life any more than the drops can be regarded as outside the ocean, and if through all this intimate connection with Deity we still continue to retain our distinct individual existence in the present world, there can indeed be no reason to conclude that in any future state of being the union with God shall absorb the personality. Pantheism, destructive as it is to nearly every belief and doctrine which Christianity holds dear, seems thus, nevertheless, disposed to extend more kindness to the faith in a future state than to most other traditional tenets. This at least may be said in its favour, that if by nature it tends to disparage Man's faith in immortality, it yet offers a loophole through which an aspiring mind can escape from the prospect of annihilation, and enter into the prophecy of an endless life. And if this may be said even of the Left Hegelianism, what shall we say of the Right? In any disparaging sense of the word, the Right Hegelianism is not pantheistic at all. It is true that here, as in the foregoing system, God is the fulness of all things. It is true that, alike in the Right as in the Left, the divine life is conceived as filling immensity with its presence, and participating in the being of every insect that flutters in the summer breeze; a world whose life was separated from the divine life would be a world for the atheist alone. But while in the system of Hegel God is all, it can never be said that all is God. There is nothing outside of Him, nothing which His presence does not fill, yet all things put together would not sum up that presence. God, in the system of Hegel, in the system of Schelling, nay, for that matter, even in the system of Spinoza, is greater than all His works, and to be thought of as existent before all; and although every one of these philosophies has from time to time been stamped with the name of pantheism, and burdened with its supposed consequence of denying immortality, it must be acknowledged by every candid mind, that even were the consequence admitted to be inevitable, the premiss on which it is based is erroneous and unfounded.

CHAPTER XI.—Page 121.

In placing Hegel on the Right, we have, in addition to other things, had regard to the fact that he allows full scope to the province of religion in the individual mind, being in this respect at the farthest possible remove from his disciple, Bruno Bauer. We have in these pages endeavoured to expound the Hegelian Trinity in its timeless sphere; we have endeavoured to explain it as it is evolved in the world of time; and we have endeavoured to view it in that reconciliation of time with eternity which is exhibited in the history of the Church. But it has occurred to us that the student might like to learn whether this Hegelian theory has any influence upon practical life,—whether it has any voice which speaks to the religious experience of each man; and therefore we shall try, as briefly as possible, to set before him a statement of Hegel's position with reference to the spiritual history of each Christian believer. Now, Christian belief in the system of Hegel has three stages, and in expounding these we shall follow the plan we have adopted throughout this treatise; that is to say, we shall pay more regard to the thing signified than to the sign or term which is used to denote it. The subject has special difficulties of its own, for it is occupied with a sphere so peculiarly inward as to require much self-study before we can even begin to examine it. Other parts of the Hegelian system may be read and understood by him who has merely studied the laws of history and examined the natural development of his own soul; but he who would interpret a theory which purports to delineate religious experience, must himself, in the heart of that experience, have already lived, and moved, and had his being. We proceed now, however, very briefly to state this theory. According to Hegel, the spiritual life of a believer in Christ begins, as it were, with the life of the body. In other words, it takes its rise in that outward and visible sphere which forms the starting-point of all human thought. As the disciple on the shores of Galilee derived his earliest nourishment from the scenes which met his eye and the words which were addressed to his ear, so the disciple of every age must begin his spiritual existence by fixing his thoughts upon those facts and verbal statements in which the religion of Christ has clothed itself. He too begins by walking in thought beside the manger of Bethlehem, and by the Lake of Gennesaret, and in the garden of Gethsemane, and under the shadow of the Cross of Calvary. He too finds his earliest joy in transcribing the very words of Holy Writ, and interpreting these words according to their most literal acceptation. The modern believer enters upon his spiritual existence by traversing the world of the past; and he traverses that world that he may find those bodily shapes and images which are shrouded from the present hour. Every man in this stage is in the position of the medieval world. He is in search of the visible cross, and the visible Jerusalem, and the visible monuments of redeeming love, and his whole life is, as it were, a series of crusades undertaken to liberate from the mists of antiquity those scenes and historical incidents which form the framework of the gospel. Our spiritual being begins with the existence of the body.

But by and by there comes a change. It came even to the first disciples. In process of time the historical scenes were withdrawn, outward contact with the Master soon ceased to exist, miraculous manifestations became ever rarer and more rare, and at last the holy city itself, which had been the pride and glory of every Jewish heart, passed into the hands of a heathen generation. The spiritual life was thus separated from the body, from the things of sense, from the facts of history, and the period of outward experience was succeeded by the season of inward reflection, the life of the body by the life of the soul. Men could no longer see Christ; they must believe in Him, must trust Him through the distance, must stretch out the hand to touch Him in the darkness; the second age was the age of faith. And the experience of the early disciples is repeated in every spiritual mind. To us, too, there comes a time when the outward framework no longer suffices, when we crave for something deeper, fuller, more satisfying. We begin to cry out for some abiding principle, something which was not merely true once, but which will always be true; and as we cannot be expected to find this experience in a moment, it is necessary we should believe in it until we have found it. Hence to us also the stage between outward sight and inward fruition is the exercise of faith, the belief in that which we cannot see, the trust in that which we are unable to trace. It may be that this stage of faith has itself been preceded by a stage of doubt; nay, in accordance with the system of Hegel, it must be so. In the Hegelian theory, everything exists only by reaction with its opposite; hence we cannot conceive that a man should arrive at faith before he has passed through a period of doubt. A faith which is not preceded by such doubt must be a purely traditional belief; in other words, the belief not in a truth, but in an authority or series of authorities by which that truth has been transmitted. The transition, therefore, from the historical to the reflective period of religious life is marked by a momentary sense of separation from God, the moorings seem lost, and we drift awhile without a helm. Yet the faith is all the more valuable from the anarchy which went before it, just as the day is all the more prized because it is a reaction from the night. In the system of Hegel, the greatest glory of the human soul is not the non-existence of evil, but the overcoming of evil. He tells us that the dictum of conscience is, 'Evil is not to be;' by which it is meant, not that sin is to have no existence, but that it is to have no continuance of existence; if evil did not exist, conscience could not utter this mandate. It is therefore in perfect accordance with the Hegelian principle, that after the eye has ceased to be satisfied with the outward scenes of Christianity, it should for a time be satisfied with nothing, but should pronounce all things to be vanity and vexation of spirit, until the inner light of faith shall compensate in some measure for the outer eye of sense, and enable the soul to believe in those realities whose outward forms it can no longer see.

Here, then, are the first two stages of Christian experience as exhibited in the system of Hegel: the age of the body and the age of the soul; the time of outward vision and the season of inward reflection; the confidence which believes because it has seen, and the trust which has not seen and yet believes. But now we come to a third and final period, which may be said to reconcile the other two; it is the period of thought or knowledge. Here we have, as it were, a restoration of direct evidence; faith ceases to exist, but merely because it has been swallowed up in sight. It is not, indeed, the first sight of external vision, not the perception of outward apparitions or the beholding of miraculous changes; that belonged to the infancy of our being, and with that infancy it has passed away for ever. The new sight is no longer external, but spiritual; not the vision of something without, but the clear perception of a principle within. Yet the vision is not less real because it is internal; it has this analogy to our earliest spiritual experience, that they both constitute sources of direct and immediate evidence. The three stages might be thus described:

Supplementary Notes.

we begin by seeing God, we pass into believing in God, and we end by knowing God. The last is unquestionably the highest; the mere recognition of one by sight is an inferior mode of acquaintance to that knowledge of his character which comes from intimacy. But while knowing is better than seeing, both knowing and seeing are sources of higher evidence than mere believing; faith is confessedly a difficult process, and the difficulty lies in this, that every act of faith implies an absence of all evidence outside its own light. Knowledge, therefore, is in one aspect a restoration of our early vision; we no longer can be said merely to believe. Faith is the human torch for the night, knowledge is the celestial sun which makes it unnecessary; when that which is perfect is come, then that which is in part is done away. We begin by adoring only the earthly Christ, the Christ after the flesh, the Christ of Galilee; this is the age when the spirit is absorbed in the body. We come next to the adoration of the ascended Jesus, the Christ in heaven, the Being who has passed from sight and can only be apprehended by faith; this is the age when the body is absorbed in the spirit. We arrive at last at a point where the Christ of earth and the Christ of heaven are worshipped in one act, where He is recognised, no longer indeed in outward form, but as yet in the most real sense present to the soul; not as the Christ beside us, nor as the Christ above us, but as something which comprehends and transcends them both; the Christ that is within us, here at length is the perfect fruit of the Divine Spirit. Such, in the system of Hegel, is the history of evangelical belief. It is for those who have passed through that experience to say whether the German philosopher has or has not accurately described its working. This, however, it is impossible to deny, that while it finds an analogy in the wider history of generic Man, it receives a strong corroboration from much of the language of Scripture. Into the proof of this our limits forbid us to enter, and it is the less necessary as the means of verifying it lie before all. Other parts of the Hegelian theory require a vast amount of external knowledge in him who would determine the measure of their truth, but he who would decide this point, if only he have a spiritual mind, needs nothing more,—no books, no travels, no researches,—for he has but to look within to discover in his own heart the light by which to read it, and according to the testimony of that light he can pronounce it false or true.

CHAPTER XII.—Page 143.

In considering the objections to the mythical theory, we have called the Pauline epistles to the Romans, Corinthians, and Galatians, the Fifth Gospel. It has long seemed to us, that should the needs of the age demand a new work on apologetics, that work should take as its basis the testimony of these epistles to the facts of the gospel history. The ground of this subject has been admirably broken by Professor Leathes in his Boyle Lecture for 1869, but even here it is little more than broken. We want in this field a new *Horæ Paulinæ*, in which the same congruity which Paley endeavoured to establish between the Pauline epistles and the Acts shall be established between the Pauline epistles and the Gospels. The inquiry will be of more interest from the fact, that since the days of Paley many of those documents which have been cited as testimonies to Christianity have been consigned to the region of doubt. The Epistle of Barnabas can no longer be ascribed to him; that of Hermas, if it belong to a man of that name, must be placed at the close of the second century; the first Epistle of Clement is more than doubtful; the Letters of Ignatius have been reduced successively from fifteen to seven, and from seven to three, and the genuineness even of the three is by no means established; the very quotations from Justin Martyr, which were thought to point conclusively to the Gospels of Matthew, Mark, and Luke, can no longer with certainty be referred to that source. When we add to this that melancholy spirit of destructive criticism which has sought to tear up by the roots the sacred writings themselves, which has denied the genuineness of the fourth Gospel, and rejected in turn nearly every book of the New Testament, from the Acts to the Apocalypse, we are more than ever constrained to seek out some sure landing-place, where we may rest without fear. Our first aim should be no longer to establish the authenticity of books, but to confirm the truth of facts; and we can only do so by the possession of a document which is admittedly written at the time of these facts. Such a document will be found in these four epistles of Paul, received alike by the orthodox and by the heretical, undenied either by the mythicism of a Strauss or by the critical acumen of a Baur of Tübingen, and only questioned for the first time by Bruno Bauer in the wanton determination to break with every vestige of the past. This solitary testimony, rejected alike by friends and foes, is not likely to injure the stability of an anchorage which has been able successfully to resist the destructive winds and waves which lent so stormy an aspect to the earlier speculations of this nineteenth century.

CHAPTER XVI.—PAGE 182.

IN one sense, nothing can be more opposite than the speculations of modern British science, and the speculations of German Hegelian thought. When Darwin promulgated his theory of development, it was received by the English world as a new contribution to materialism, and as itself the legitimate progeny of that materialism which had long constituted the tendency of science in this country. Nor are we for a moment disposed to deny that the first aspect of this development theory was decidedly materialistic. The truth is, that as it passes from one hand to another it seems ever increasingly to be deserting its own standpoint,—becoming less English and more German. Darwin was not its originator, and before it came into his hands it had already passed through its more repulsive stages. It was transplanted from a French soil. Its earliest votary was Lamarck, and with him, so far as we can gather, the primal germ of all things is mere matter. In the *Vestiges of Creation*, a book which at its appearance attracted much attention and excited some alarm, the view is very little higher; matter is still the germ, only it seems to be dressed in more beautiful attributes, and this lends to the work a certain literary charm. In Darwinism properly so called we get a step in advance of either, for here the primal object which evolves itself throughout the ages into forms so many and so varied is no longer mere matter, but actual life. Up to this time life was itself a part of the evolution; it is now the principle of the evolution. In the hands of Alfred Wallace, one of Darwin's disciples, the theory has assumed a garb more spiritual still; here we have not mere matter, nor yet even mere life, but a life that is intelligent,—in other words, a principle of thought which expresses in outward action the beauty and the harmony that lie within itself. Now is it not just at this point that we are entitled to look for something like an amalgamation between English and German thought? The theory of *The Vestiges* was diametrically opposed to that of Hegel, inasmuch as the one rested on a material and the other on a spiritual basis. The theory of Darwin was also opposed to that of Hegel, inasmuch as the one started from mere life, and the other from thinking intelligence; but beneath their opposition, and deeper than their difference, there was one thought common to all the three—the idea of development. The followers of *The Vestiges* and the followers of Darwin in England would have shaken hands with those of Hegel in Germany over this one article of peace; they all looked upon this universe as a gradual evolution from the small to the great, from the germ to the completed structure; and the only difference was, that while the English men of science assigned this evolution to finite agency, the German theologians imputed it to the operation of a divine life which had been breathed into His works by the Infinite Spirit. In the form of the theory adopted by Alfred Wallace, this difference already begins to disappear; nature casts off the aspect of a mere dead mechanism, moved by inevitable laws—casts off even that higher aspect of a vital spark which by its own unconscious intensity spreads out into a great fire of being; the mechanical is exchanged for the intellectual, the vital for the mental force. Nature is presented to us as the repository of a great divine life, which, starting indeed from small beginnings, and working originally upon slender materials, contains yet within itself all possibilities, however infinite. The prospective whole is already included in the germ, and that which is to be evolved in time is already involved in eternal thought. The attributes of mind are no longer merely the latest fruit on the tree of development; they are themselves the very seed from which that tree has grown, the primal basis on which the whole future structure must repose, —at once the beginning and origination of all that lives, and moves, and has its being.

Such is one of the most recent phases which the theory of development has assumed; and as this form of it is also the product of British science, its very existence seems to indicate that science has found materialism an inadequate foundation. Indeed, it is our decided conviction that the reign of materialism in this country has long since passed its zenith. Its course is not difficult to trace. It perhaps may be said to have derived its earliest impulse from the prevalence of Locke's philosophy; it received a still greater accession from the theory of Hartley's vibrations; it rose into prominence in the philosophy of Dr. Priestley; and it was culminated in that English adaptation of Lamarck's creed adopted in the *Vestiges of Creation*. Here, so far as we can observe, its influence has paused. Steadily and surely the current seems changing, and even the scientific mind is recoiling from the illuminism of the last century. We have still amongst us those who make it their province to exhibit science in its antagonism to revelation. Yet it is surely a favourable sign that even the names most associated with this antagonism would repudiate the charge of materialism. We are inclined, therefore, to conclude that the purely external standpoint is a stage surmounted; and as no age of the world exactly repeats itself, we see no reason to believe that it will ever be restored. What may be the new direction of events it would be idle to speculate, but the fact of movement is itself an indication of life, and we cannot but hope that the reaction in the heart of British science is the transition into an atmosphere which shall be loftier and more pure.

INDEX.

BAUER, Bruno, 124, 131, 146.
Baur, F. C., of Tübingen, 131, 148–155 (*d.* 1860).
Belgham, 175.
Bengel, 176 (*d.* 1751).
Böhme, Jacob, 85 (*d.* 1624).
Bolingbroke, 141 (*d.* 1751).
Branez, 131.
Butler, 140.

CHUBB, 141 (*d.* 1747).
Clarke, 175 (*d.* 1729).
Collins, 141 (*d.* 1729).
Comte, 77, 124, 171 (*d.* 1858).

D'ALEMBERT, 5.
Daub, 98, 131 (*d.* 1836).
Delitzsch, 70, 71.
Des Cartes, 5 (*d.* 1650).
De Wette, 35, 61 (*d.* 1851).
Diderot, 5 (*d.* 1784).
Dœderlin, 7 (*d.* 1792).
Dorner, 1, 61, 62, 65, 66, 67, 68, 132.

EBERHARD, 7 (*d.* 1809).
Ebrard, 69–71.
Erdmann, 131.
Ewald, 61, 66, 160–163.

FEURBACH, 123, 130 (*d.* 1872).
Fichte, John Gottlieb, 32, 72–81, 83, 179 (*d.* 1814).
Fichte, J. H., 131.
Fischer, 131.

GESS, 68.
Gieseler, 1 (*d.* 1854).
Goschel, 132, 133.

HAGENBACH, 1.
Harris, 176.
Hase, 61, 66.
Hegel, 14, 18, 19, 36, 62, 66, 71, 82–119, 131, 132, 134, 179, 181 (*d.* 1832).
Hitzig, 131.
Hume, 178, 179 (*d.* 1776).
Huxley, 168.

JACOBI, 35 (*d.* 1819).
Jerusalem, 8.

KANT, 5, 9, 11–32, 40, 41, 47, 53, 65, 72, 73, 83, 156, 178, 179 (*d.* 1804).
Keim, 162.

LANGE, 61, 62, 66, 68, 132.
Leibnitz, 5 (*d.* 1716).
Less, 8.
Liebner, 66, 132.
Löffler, 7.
Lücke, 61 (*d.* 1855).

MARHEINECKE, 98, 131 (*d.* 1846).
Martensen, 61, 62, 66, 67, 132.
Michelet, 131.
Mill, John Stuart, 9, 168 (*d.* 1873).
Miller, 8.
Mosheim, 1 (*d.* 1755).
Müller, Julius, 64, 65, 66.

NEANDER, 1, 61 (*d.* 1850).
Nitzsch, 61.
Nobel, 131.
Nosselt, 8.

OETINGER, 85, 176 (*d.* 1782).

Index.

Olshausen, 63 (*d.* 1839).
Osiander, 85 (*d.* 1552).

PALEY, 9, 180 (*d.* 1805).
Paulus, 153, 158, 159, 161, 162 (*d.* 1851).
Priestley, 175 (*d.* 1804).

RENAN, Ernest, 153, 157–159, 161, 162, 163.
Rosencranz, 108, 131.
Rothe, 61, 63, 66, 68, 132 (*d.* 1867).
Ruysbroeck, 3, 173 (*d.* 1381).

SCHALLER, 131.
Schelling, 36, 131, 179 (*d.* 1854).
Schenkel, 157–159, 161, 162.
Schlegel, 34, 179 (*d.* 1810).
Schleiermacher, 34–71, 72, 112, 132, 134, 135, 165, 169, 179 (*d.* 1834).
Schwegler, 89, 150.
Schweizer, 60, 61, 66.
Scotus, John Erigena, 85.

Semler, 8, 9 (*d.* 1791).
Spalding, 8.
Staupitz, 3.
Steinbart, 7.
Strauss, 36, 53, 56, 124, 131, 134–145, 164–171 (*d.* 1873).

TAULER, 3, 173.
Tholuck, 60, 70, 71.
Thomasius, 66, 68.
Tœlner, 7.
Twesten, 61.

ULLMANN, 61, 66.

VATCHE, 131.

WEGSCHEIDER, 152, 159 (*d.* 1849).
Weisse, 62, 63, 66, 131.
Wesel, 3.
Wesley, 176 (*d.* 1791).
Whitby, 175.
Whitefield, 176.
Wickliffe, 173 (*d.* 1384).

www.ingramcontent.com/pod-product-compliance
Lightning Source LLC
Chambersburg PA
CBHW051049160426
43193CB00010B/1114